P9-CRV-216

THE
INTERIOR
CASTLE
SAINT
TERESA
OF
AVILA

THE INTERIOR CASTLE
SAINT TERESA OF AVILA

Translated into modern English
and abridged for accessibility
by John Venard OCD

E. J. DWYER
Sydney • Philadelphia

HICKSVILLE PUBLIC LIBRARY
169 JERUSALEM AVE.
HICKSVILLE, N.Y.

The Interior Castle
This edition published 1988 by
E.J. Dwyer Pty Ltd
Unit 3, 32-72 Alice Street
Newtown NSW 2042
Australia

E.J. Dwyer Pty Ltd
2772 Country Club Road
Philadelphia PA 19131
U.S.A.

© 1988, John Venard, O.C.D.
First published in 1980, reprinted in 1985, reprinted in 1989.

This book is copyright. Apart from any fair dealing for the purposes of
private study, research, criticism or review, as permitted under the
Copyright Act, no part may be reproduced by any process without
written permission. Inquiries should be addressed to the publishers.

National Library of Australia
Cataloguing-in-Publication data
Teresa, of Avila, Saint, 1515-1582.
    (Moradas. English). The interior castle.

    Abridged version
    ISBN 0 85574 180 5.

    1. Spiritual life — Catholic authors.
    I. Venard, John. II. Title. III:
    Moradas. English.

248.4'82

Library of Congress Cataloging-in-Publication data
Teresa, of Avila, Saint, 1515-1582.
    (Moradas. English.)
    The interior castle/Saint Teresa of Avila; translated into modern
    English and abridged for accessibility by John Venard.
        p.   cm.
    Translation of: Las moradas.
    ISBN 0-85574-180-5

    1. Spiritual life — Catholic authors — Early works to 1800.
    I. Venard, John. II. Title

BX2179.T4M63 1988
248.4'82 — dc19   88-25087
                                                              CIP

Nihil Obstat: Most Reverend Julio X. Labayen, O.C.D.
                Prelate Ordinary of Infanta
Imprimatur: Very Reverend Fr. Finian Monahan, O.C.D.
                Superior General, Order of Discalced Carmelites

Typeset by Love Computer Typesetting Pty Ltd, Sydney

Printed and bound in Australia by
Southwood Press Pty Limited, Marrickville, NSW

248.482
J

Contents

Seventh Mansions

Jesus   105

Analytical Outline of Certain Basic Stages in the Life of Teresa

Date	External Life	Writings	Psychological Development	Spiritual Life
1515	March 28: birth in Avila, Spain.		Predominance of emotional life.	Childhood fervor.
1521				Takes the Blessed Virgin as her mother.
1528	Death of Teresa's mother.		Frivolity.	Repents of her frivolity and her great fear of losing her soul.
1531	Enrolls as a boarding student at the Convent of Our Lady of Grace in Avila.		Sentimental attachment to Doña María Briceño; impressed by her pious examples; decides to be a nun.	
1536	Enters the Carmelite Order in the Incarnation convent, Avila.		Romantic notions of convent life.	First fervor as a nun.
1537	Professed as a nun by taking the religious vows.		Struggles to overcome emotions; suffers nervous fatigue.	
1538	Illness; granted permission by her religious superiors to stay with her sister Maria while she takes the cure; enroute she visits her uncle, Pedro.		Reads spiritual writings to Don Pedro and is deeply impressed by them and by him.	Accepts illness with fortitude; her devotion to St. Joseph assumes definite form.
1540	Returns to the Incarnation convent.		Returns to superficial living.	Renounces the practice of prayer from a false notion of humility.
1543	Death of Teresa's father.			Seeks spiritual direction from Vincent Barron, O.P.
1554			Makes great progress toward maturity through reading St. Augustine's Confessions.	Experiences definitive conversion and growth in prayer.

Date	External Life	Writings	Psychological Development	Spiritual Life
1556?				First rapture.
1558?				First rapture.
1559				June 29: first intellectual vision of the Humanity of Christ.
1560	September: takes the first steps toward the Reform, but it met with failure.	First spiritual relation written to Father Pedro Ibañez, O.P.		Vision of hell (*Life*, Chapter 32); various visions of Humanity of Christ; makes a vow of greater perfection.
1561				August 15: vision in which she is assured of spiritual cleanliness (*Life*, Chapter 33).
1562	August 24: Inauguration of the Carmelite Reform by foundation of the Convent of San José in Avila.	First draft of her *Life* and spiritual relation No. 2 to Ibañez.		Experiences one of several transverberations of her heart; her spiritual espousal (*Life*, Chapter 29).
1566		First version of *The Way of Perfection*; spiritual relation No. 3.		
1567	Founds convent at Medina del Campo; takes steps to extend the Reform to the Carmelite friars.			
1568	Founds convents in Malagón and Valladolid; with her help the friars establish a monastery in Duruelo.			
1569	Founds convents in Toledo and Pastrana.	Composes *Exclamations of the Soul to God* and the second version of *The Way of Perfection*.		

Date	External Life	Writings	Psychological Development	Spiritual Life
1570	Founds convent in Salamanca.			Experiences steps necessary to the spiritual marriage (*Life*, Chapter 39); spiritual relations No. 15 and 16.
1571	Founds convent in Alba de Tormes; from October 1571 to October 1574 is Prioress of the Incarnation convent in Avila.			
1572				November 18: spiritual marriage.
1573		Begins writing the *Foundations* (Chapters 1–9).		
1574	Founds convent in Segovia.	Continues *Foundations* (Chapters 10–19).		
1575	Founds convents in Beas and Sevilla.			Makes a vow of obedience to Father Gratian.
1576		Completes *Foundations* (Chapters 20–27).		
1577	Great opposition to the Reform.	Composes *The Interior Castle*.		
1579	Persecution abates.			
1580	Learns that Pope Gregory III has permitted the Reform to have its own jurisdiction; founds convents in Villanueva de la Jar and Palencia.	Makes certain changes in the text of *The Interior Castle*.		
1581	Founds convent in Soria.			
1582	Founds convent in Burgos; dies on October 4 in Alba de Tormes.	Makes final additions to *Foundations* (Chapters 26–31).		

St. Teresa of Avila
Biographical Note

Teresa de Cepeda y Ahumada was born on the Wednesday of Holy Week, 28 March 1515, at Avila. Her grandfather had adopted the Jewish religion, but returned to the Catholic faith. She grew up in a devotly Catholic home and we find her at the age of six setting off with her brother Rodrigo to the land of the Moors "to merit the blessings of heaven as quickly as possible and to see God" by winning the crown of martyrdom.

Her mother died when Teresa was thirteen and in her desolation she took the Blessed Virgin for her mother. But richly endowed as she was with wit, beauty and wisdom, the years following were, as she tells us, "given over to vanities". She was a very normal fun-loving teenager but her father, concerned about certain dubious friendships she had made, enrolled her as a boarder at the local Augustinian convent. Here she was befriended by a gentle nun under whose influence she began to think of entering the convent, but her health declined and she returned home.

During her convalescence she spent some time with her uncle Pedro and in reading his spiritual books aloud to him. Despite her initial lack of enthusiasm for the task she became intrested and finally captivated. This new interest in the spiritual life led her, despite the repugnance she still felt to be religious life, to think seriously again of entering the convent. This she did, stealing away quietly very early one morning (her father had refused permission) to the Carmelite Convent of the Incarnation, where the nuns were awaiting her. She was in her twenty-first year.

Although she was happy at the Incarnation her health broke down, so badly that her life was despaired of and she was actually thought to be dead. Funeral arrangements were made; her eyes were sealed with wax, according to the custom of the time, and she would have been buried except for the stubborn insistence of her father. She recovered, attributing her cure to St. Joseph, but it was a slow and painful recovery, for she was in a state of semiparalysis for nearly three years, and she was never again to know a day completely free from sickness.

During this time of convalescence she renewed contact with her uncle and he gave her a book on mystical prayer, *The Third Alphabet of Osuna*.

In it she discovered how to practice mental prayer, and as she had already had some experience of passive prayer, without understanding clearly what was happening, this book enlightened her as to the nature of these experiences. She had no other guide for the next twenty years; those from whom she sought help were incapable of guiding her and it was only in the year 1560 that, meeting St. Peter of Alcantara in Avila, she received assurance and encouragement. This holy Franciscan was the first of a long line of remarkable spiritual guides — Jesuits, Dominicans, Carmelites, Augustinians — who subsequently guided her in her mystical journey to the heights of divine union.

Teresa became dissatisfied with the way of life at the Incarnation. Enclosure was not at all strict and contact with the outside world was virtually unrestricted; Teresa with her expansive personality had a constant stream of visitors. But she also felt that God was calling her to a more comtemplative kind of life and there began within her an intense struggle between opposing attractions. She was powerfully drawn to a life of close union with God, but loath to give up the pastimes of the world and social contacts, which she knew were frivolous and distracting. Grace triumphed and she decided, with a few companions, to leave the Incarnation and found a strictly enclosed convent. This foundation, the Carmelite Convent of St. Joseph at Avila, founded 24 August 1562, when Teresa was forty-seven, was the first of many foundations of the Discalced Carmelite Reform.

These foundations, sixteen in all, from Burgos in the north to Sevilla in the south of Spain, were to entail incredible hardship and contradiction. But her indomitable spirit prevailed; not only did she place the new order of nuns on a sound footing but she also inaugurated and founded the order of Discalced Carmelite Friars. She persuaded a Carmelite friar of the Ancient Order, who would become St. John of the Cross, to join the Reform and become the first Discalced Carelite Father. He with two companions made the first foundation of the friars at Duruelo in 1568.

While at St. Joseph's, Avila, in 1562, St. Teresa, at the behest of her confessors, began to write down an account of her spiritual life. Although never intended for publication, this, her first work, became known as the *Life*. It is partly autobiographical, but it is primarily a book on prayer and the account of her own special graces from God, intended only for the small group of her spiritual advisers. It was published only after her death. Some would consider it her greatest work; it contains a precious little treatise of eleven chapters on prayer, the Four Waters. It was completed in 1565 and almost immediately she began, at the earnest request of her Carmelite daughters, a book on prayer which became known as *The Way of Perfection*: the "little book" as she called it. In it she encourages all to attain the "living water" of contemplative prayer; the last section of the book, Chapters 27 to 42, is devoted to a prayerful commentary on the Our Father. Besides eight minor works, some thirty poems and over four hundred letters she wrote a lively narrative of her work as foundress, entitled the *Foundations*. Chapter 5 of this book should be read by those who need to resolve the tension arising from activity and contemplation. The last and perhaps the greatest of her works was written in 1577, *The Interior Castle*, a profound reflection on the soul's progressive discovery, through seven stages, or "Mansions", of the divine indwelling.

St. Teresa died on the feast of St. Francis, to who she had a special devotion. Her last foundation, Burgos, had caused her great suffering. She was physically exhausted and she had to endure hostility and rejection even from her closest friends and associates. She died peacefully, repeating quietly "O God, a contrite and humble heart you will not despire" and , just before her death, "I die, a daughter of the Church".

A faithful and loving daughter of the Church, indeed; she was canonized on 12 March 1622, along with Sts. Ignatius, Francis Xavier and Isidore. On 27 September 1970 she was proclaimed, along with St. Catherine of Siena, Doctor of the Church, by Pope Paul VI. It was fitting; Pope Pius X had said of her: "So great has been her influence that it is second only to that of the greatest Fathers and Doctors of the Church, if indeed it is second to them."

Introduction

The *Interior Castle* was written in 1577, five years before St. Teresa's death. It is generally considered the greatest of her works, and we have good evidence for thinking that she considered it so herself. She had already written the *Life* in 1562, a résumé of her interior life, and *The Way of Perfection*, completed in 1569, with its emphasis on the fundamental virtues as a preparation for the mystical life.

Building on the great foundations of prayer already laid in these two works, the sacred Humanity of the Risen Christ and the Fatherhood of Good, she now makes the Indwelling of the Blessed Trinity her central theme. She leads us through the Mansions to contemplation as we progress in "entering within"; from knowledge in pure faith of this mystery, to a lived and living experience, still in faith, of the presence of the three divine Persons within us.

The first three Mansions are the preparatory, ascetical stages of active prayer and self-discipline in the practice of the everyday virtues. The Fourth Mansion is a transitional stage. The Fifth, Sixth and Seventh Mansions treat specifically of the mystical life of infused contemplation, of passive prayer and of the degrees of union with God culminating in the spiritual marriage, a grace given to St. Teresa in 1572. From that time she enjoyed uninterrupted communion with the Blessed Trinity.

She encourages us all to come by this way; not necessarily by the way of the extraordinary graces, or by the "favors" she describes in these Mansions, but by the sure Way, Christ — the Way, the Truth, and the Life — until in response to God's love we arrive at total conformity of our wills with the will of God. This is the highest contemplation, and it will find its expression in works: the service of others, charity, the apostolate.

St. Teresa's approach to prayer is thoroughly and completely scriptural. *The Interior Castle* is, to use her own words, simply a commentary of our Lord's words at the Last Supper (John 14:23). Allowing herself some liberty with the actual text, she says:

> All three Persons communicate themselves to the soul, and speak to it, explaining the words of the Gospel, that "He and the Father and the Holy Spirit will come to dwell with the soul which loves Him and keeps His commandments" (Seventh Mansions, Chapter 1).

Contemplation, in the words of Hans von Balthasar, "must be conceived Biblically." St. Teresa is contemporary in this as in all else connected with her teaching on prayer. She speaks to us in the twentieth century as though she were aware of our difficulties, especially of the urgency of our need to pray in this our time. We have to learn to "enter within," finding God "in the little heaven of our own souls." St. Teresa knows every step of the way there. She is a sure and sympathetic guide; she speaks a language we can all understand.

However, the writings of St. Teresa present certain difficulties to the modern reader.

1.   There seems to be a lack of planning in the presentation. There are many digressions, a wandering from the main theme, a lack of precision in developing the imagery of, for example, the castle, the mansions, the silkworm. This results in confusion and difficulty in following the Saint's line of thought and her teaching on prayer.

Many fail to persevere in reading the whole text, hence this book. It is hoped that St. Teresa's thought will come through clearly, as those passages not directly connected with her teaching on prayer have been omitted, so that the essential message is more readily assimilated, in a format easily accessible to those who wish to take St. Teresa as their guide in the way of prayer. The order of chapters, and the Saint's thought-sequence, have been retained. This book is not simply a series of excerpts or quotations.

2.   At first sight, it appears that there is, in the writings of St. Teresa, undue emphasis on ecstasies, visions and raptures, as though these are considered necessary to be really prayerful, really contemplative.

A careful reading of the text reveals that St. Teresa, along with St. John of the Cross, thinks and teaches the exact opposite. She warns us repeatedly that these extraordinary manifestations and favors are not necessary, and that we are not to desire them or to think that holiness consists in them. If God allows them, they can be of great value, but they are not in themselves a sign of holiness and there can be genuine contemplation without them.

For St. Teresa the sign of the true contemplative is to say with Christ, "Thy will be done." It must be remembered that St. Teresa is describing her own experiences. She speaks from the empirical point of view and never merely theorizes about prayer.

3.   There seems to be emphasis only on personal prayer, on being alone with God. What of community prayer, "shared" prayer? Those who are familiar with prayer groups and charismatic assemblies may feel that there is an almost selfish preoccupation with "oneself and God."

St. Teresa was fully aware of the community dimension of prayer, but she places the emphasis very firmly on its personal aspects in her writings. She knew very well that if we are to achieve community, or to pray well in community, we must have a close and personal relationship with God, and that this is the way to dispose ourselves to pray with and live with others; this applies especially to liturgical prayer.

The desire to be "alone with the Alone" is in no way contradictory to sharing with others in prayer. St. Teresa in fact achieved something of a breakthrough in the notion of contemplation in the Church; she enriched the concept of "aloneness" with an apostolic dimension. The expression in *Perfectae Caritatis* (the document on Religious Life in Vatican II) — "combining contemplation with apostolic love" — fits St. Teresa's ideal of contemplation perfectly. Contemplation is not for oneself, but for others, for the Church and for those who are called to it, an apostolate and vocation in itself.

Those who have experience of prayer groups will readily acknowledge that they become more aware, as a result of the experience, of the need of a more personal, intensified prayer life. They will find a sure guide in St. Teresa.

4. Some may be disappointed that there seems to be no clear-cut "method of prayer" outlined in *The Interior Castle*.

The reason for this is that, for St. Teresa, prayer is a way of life and she is concerned primarily with what we are before God. Progress in love of God goes hand in hand with the progressive discovery of God-within-us, along with the realization, by the grace of the Holy Spirit, that we are one with the Risen Christ, since we are made in the image and likeness of God (First Mansions, Chapter 1).

Prayer is our personal expression of a love relationship. We pass from awareness of this relationship to response in faith and love, coming to "fullness of maturity in Christ" as intimacy with God deepens. Prayer, in St. Teresa's view, does not consist in much thinking, or in many words, but in "loving much."

There is a Carmelite method of prayer based on Chapter 26 in *The Way of Perfection*, which may be summed up in St. Teresa's words:

I am not asking you now to think of Him [Christ], or form numerous conceptions of Him, or make long and subtle meditations with the understanding. I am asking you only to look at Him.

So we learn to practice "recollection," concentrating on the person of the Risen Christ within us, not thinking in detail of the events of His Life, Passion, Death, Resurrection (though this will be necessary in the beginning), but rather communing in love with Him, with His person, in these mysteries. Or we can pray the Our Father, thus arriving at the highest contemplation, or we can remember God-within-us and lovingly commune with the three divine Persons. All this goes hand in hand with prayerful, meditative reading of the Scriptures, which is, in itself, according to St. Teresa, a sufficient "method" and a necessary food for the "royal road" of prayer.

The purpose of this book will be achieved if more and more people will be encouraged to set out on this "divine journey" with St. Teresa, and read her works in their entirety.

First Mansions
(Two Chapters)

1 The beauty and dignity of the soul.

The soul seems to me
to be like a castle,
made of a single diamond
or of very clear crystal
in which there are many rooms,
just as in heaven
there are many mansions.

The soul of the just man
is nothing but a paradise,
in which God takes His delight;
God, who is "a King so mighty,
so wise, so pure, so good."

We can no more understand
the beauty of the soul
than we can God himself.
He created us
"in His own image and likeness."
So it is impossible to imagine it
and useless to fatigue ourselves in trying.

The very fact
that His Majesty says it is made in His image
means that we can hardly form any conception
of the soul's great dignity and beauty.

It is a great shame
not to know who we are in these terms.
We become like a person
who has no idea who he is,
who his father and mother are,

from what country he came.
We seldom consider what it means,
to be created in the image and likeness of God,
because all our interest is centered
in the rough setting of the diamond,
and in the outer wall of the castle;
that is to say, in these bodies of ours.

This castle contains many Mansions,
above, below, at each side;
and in the center and midst of them all,
is the chiefest Mansion,
where the most secret things
pass between God and the soul.

It is good for us
to think of the goodness of God
in thus taking up His dwelling in us;
just as it is good for us
to think of the joys of heaven.
It is not true humility
to think that God
could not manifest His goodness
and power in us in that way.
He grants favors of this kind,
not because those who receive them
are holier than others,
but to manifest His power and greatness.

Let us enter the castle.
But how can we enter it,
since we ourselves are the castle?
We must remember
that there are many ways
of "being" in a place.
We enter within ourselves.

Souls without prayer are like people
whose bodies or limbs are paralyzed.
Some souls are so infirm,
and so accustomed

to busying themselves with outside affairs,
that nothing can be done for them;
they seem incapable
of entering within themselves at all.

They have grown so accustomed
to living among the reptiles and other creatures
to be found in the outer court of the castle
that they almost become like them;
they are by nature richly endowed,
since they have the power
of holding converse with God himself,
but nothing can be done for them.
Unless they remedy this situation,
they will become like Lot's wife —
pillars of salt,
for not looking within themselves.
The door of the castle is prayer and meditation;
not only mental prayer, but vocal, too;
for if it is prayer at all,
it must be accompanied by meditation.

Other souls enter the castle;
they are absorbed in worldly affairs,
but their desires are good.
They sometimes, but infrequently,
commend themselves to our Lord;
sometimes, not often,
they think about the state of their souls.
A few times a month, maybe;
they are preoccupied with their attachments
and worldly affairs.

From time to time
they shake themselves free of them;
eventually they get into the rooms of the first floor,
but so many reptiles enter with them
that they cannot appreciate
the beauty of the castle,
or find any peace in it.

Still, they have done a great deal
by entering at all.

This, then, is the beginning;
the prayer of the beginners,
the "door of entry into the castle."
The soul is on the way to divine intimacy.

2 The hideousness of a soul in mortal sin; self-knowledge.

Let us consider the state of the castle,
so beautiful and resplendent,
this Orient pearl, this tree of life,
planted in the living water of life,
namely, in God.

When the soul falls into mortal sin,
no thicker darkness exists.
Although the Sun himself
is still there in the center of the soul,
it is as if He were not there;
the soul has no participation in Him,
though it is capable of enjoying Him.
The soul will find profit in nothing;
none of the good works it does
will be of any avail to win it glory;
for they do not have their origin
in that First Principle, God,
through whom alone our virtue is true virtue.
It is separated from Him,
since the intention of the person
is not to please Him,
but the devil (in committing the sin).

Just as all the streamlets
flowing from a clear spring
are as clear as the spring itself,
so the works of a soul in grace
are pleasing in the eyes
both of God and of men,
since they proceed from the spring of life.
The soul in mortal sin,

rooted in a pool of pitch-black, evil-smelling water,
produces nothing but misery and filth.

The spring,
or the brilliant sun
which is the center of the soul,
does not lose its splendor and beauty;
it is as though
a thick black cloth were to be placed
over a crystal in the sunshine.

There is no evil as great as this.
Would that all souls
redeemed by Jesus Christ
would understand their natures,
and strive to remove the pitch
which blackens the crystal!
A person to whom God revealed
what a soul was like
which committed mortal sin
said that she had learned two things;
first, a great fear of ever offending Him;
second, she found it a mirror of humility,
for she learned that any good we do
has its source, not in ourselves,
but rather in that spring
where this tree, which is the soul,
is planted.
Without God's help, we are powerless.
Whenever she did a good action,
she praised God,
never giving a thought to herself.

Returning to the Mansions in the castle;
do not think of them as arranged in a row,
but fix your mind on the center,
the room or palace occupied by the King.
Think of the palmito,
with many outer rinds
surrounding the savory part within.

The soul is thought of, rightly,
as spacious and lofty,
and the Sun, which is the palace,
reaches every part of it.
It is very important
that no soul which practices prayer,
little or much,
should be subjected to undue constraint
or limitation.
It must not be compelled
to remain for a long time in one single room,
except, perhaps, that of self-knowledge.

How necessary that is!
Self-knowledge is necessary,
no matter how high the state of the soul,
and it must never neglect it.
Humility must ever be doing its work
like a bee making its honey in the hive;
without humility all is lost.
But sometimes
the soul must emerge from self-knowledge
and soar aloft in meditation
on the greatness and majesty of its God.
Thus it will realize its own baseness
rather than in thinking about itself.
We shall reach much greater heights of virtue
by thinking of the virtue of God
than if we stay in our own little plot of ground
and tie ourselves down to it completely.

Nothing matters more than humility;
if we were raised right up to the heavens,
we should never relax our cultivation of it;
we shall never succeed in knowing ourselves,
unless we seek to know God,
thinking of His greatness,
our own baseness;
of His purity, our own foulness;
of His humility, our own pride.

There are two advantages in this:
first, anything that is white
looks very much whiter
against something black;
second, our understanding and will
become nobler and readier
to embrace all that is good.
As long as we are buried
in the wretchedness of our earthly nature
we will never disengage ourselves
from the slough of cowardice,
pusillanimity, and fear.

We will rise above asking such questions as,
"Are people looking at me, or not?"
"Is pride impelling me to do this?"
"Can anyone as wretched as I
engage in so lofty an exercise of prayer?"
And so on.

This is the way the devil ruins souls.
They think these misgivings arise from humility,
whereas they come from lack of humility
and self-knowledge.
Let us stop thinking about ourselves,
and set our eyes upon Christ our God,
from whom we shall learn true humility,
and also upon the Saints.
Although we are speaking here
only about the First Mansion,
it contains riches of great price,
and to elude the reptiles at this stage
is certainly to go farther.

The many legions of evil spirits
in each of the many rooms
try to prevent souls
who enter with good intentions
from passing from one to another;
the devil is less successful
in the later Mansions, but here,

as the soul is still absorbed
in worldly affairs, pleasures and ambitions,
the faculties and senses have no power to resist,
and are easily vanquished.
These souls should, at every opportunity,
repair to His Majesty,
to the Blessed Mother, and to the Saints.

Our help in every state of life, indeed,
should come from God.
The light which comes
from the palace occupied by the King
hardly enters these First Mansions at all;
not that they are dark,
but the light is obscured by many things;
the soul cannot open its eyes to the light,
owing to its absorption in worldy things,
and being deeply immersed in possessions
and concern for honors and business.

It is unable to gaze at the beauty of the castle,
and seems quite unable
to free itself of impediments.
So anyone wishing to enter the Second Mansion
must put aside
all unnecessary affairs and business.
This is imperative
for those who hope to enter the principal Mansion.

As for us Carmelites,
as far as outward things are concerned,
we are free; but let us be free
as regards inward things, too;
beware, especially, of cares
which have nothing to do with you.
Be on the watch always
against the devil's wiles.

The devil works like a noiseless file.
For example,
it is his work, when a sister,

contrary to obedience, ruins her health
through penance forbidden to her;
or when a sister,
inspired with the desire for perfection,
thinks any little fault of her sisters
a serious failure, and runs to the Prioress;
she is unable to see her own faults,
despite her good intentions.

The devil's aim in this
is to bring about a cooling of charity and love
among the sisters.
Let us realize
that true perfection consists
in the love of God and our neighbor,
and the more nearly perfect
is our observance of these commandments,
the nearer to perfection we shall be.
Our entire Rule and Constitutions
are nothing but means
which enable us to do this more perfectly.
Let us refrain from indiscreet zeal.

This mutual love is so important;
if the soul goes about
looking for imaginary imperfections,
it may lose its own peace of mind
and disturb others.

Second Mansions

1 The great importance of perseverance.

These souls have begun to practice prayer
and realize the importance
of not remaining in the First Mansions;
but they are not resolute enough
to leave those Mansions,
and will not avoid occasions of sin.
Yet it is a great mercy
that they realize their state.
This realization
and the efforts they have to make
cause them much more distress
than that of souls in the First Mansions.

As they gradually get nearer
to the place where His Majesty dwells,
they understand the Lord
when He calls them,
and He becomes
a very good Neighbor to them.
Despite our worldliness
and preoccupation with business
and pleasure, and consequent sins,
and rising up again,
this Lord of ours
is so anxious that we should desire Him
and strive after His companionship
that He calls us ceaselessly,
time after time, to approach Him;
His voice is so sweet
that the poor soul really suffers
at not being able to do His will.

When I say "speak to us"
I mean that He appeals to us
through the conversations of good people,
through sermons, or reading good books;
and in many other ways
He speaks in sickness and trials,
and in the truths we learn in prayer;
however feeble such prayers are,
God values them highly.
Do not be disconsolate
if you do not respond immediately
to His Majesty's call;
He is prepared to wait for many days,
even many years,
especially when He sees
you are persevering and have good desires.
The devil becomes very active;
the soul, aware of the struggle, suffers much;
the devils pretend
that earthly pleasures are almost eternal;
they remind the soul of the esteem
in which it is held in the world,
of friends, relatives,
of the way in which health is endangered
by the penance
which the soul always does in this Mansion.
The devils cause the soul great confusion;
it is distressed, not knowing
whether it ought to proceed farther,
or return to the room where it was before.
Reason, however, tells it
how slight are earthly things in value;
faith instructs it as to what it must do,
memory reminds it
how all things come to an end.
The will shows it
how its true Lover never leaves it;
and the understanding shows it
how outside the castle
there is neither security nor peace;
that it has a home of its own

in which it has a Host
who will put all good things into its possession.
Let it not, then, go astray,
like the Prodigal Son.

These reflections vanquish the devils.
But so dead is our faith
that we desire to see more than faith tells us;
though we see clearly
that people who pursue these things
meet with nothing but misfortune.
The soul will certainly suffer
great trials at this time.

Here the soul needs God's help,
and the help of souls
who have made greater progress.
Especially let him have a fixed resolve
not to lose his life and his peace,
and everything he can offer
rather than return to the first room;
if he has this fixed determination,
the devil will soon cease troubling him.
He should not be like
the irresolute followers of Gideon,
but strong;
for he is going forth to fight,
and there are no better weapons
than the Cross.

It is important to remember
that at the beginning
one must not think of spiritual favors;
this is to build on sand.
Rather we should embrace the Cross,
and be ashamed
to be wanting consolations in prayer,
and complaining about periods of aridity.

Embrace the Cross, rather;
it is that of your Spouse;

the most perfect freedom
comes from bearing the cross of suffering.
All else is of secondary importance.
Simply thank the Lord
if He gives you consolation.

You may think
that if God gives you favors in prayer
you will be then strong in resisting trials.
Leave it to God;
we know not what we ask,
and it is not for us to advise God.
All that the beginner in prayer has to do —
and it must not be forgotten —
is to labor,
and to be resolute,
and prepare himself with the will of God.
This comprises the very greatest perfection
which can be attained on the spiritual road.

The more perfectly a person practices it,
the more he will receive of the Lord
and the greater progress he will make;
no need of strange jargon
or of dabbling in things we know nothing about.
Our entire welfare
is in doing what I have said.
It is sometimes the Lord's will
that we should be persecuted
and afflicted by evil thoughts
which we cannot cast out,
and also by aridities;
sometimes he allows the reptiles to bite us,
so that we may learn to be on our guard
and see if we are really grieved
at offending Him.

If, then, you sometimes fall,
do not lose heart, or cease striving,
for even out of your fall
God will draw good.

Let us see to it
that this war within us must cease;
we must come back to recollection.
The faculties are to be stilled,
and peace must reign;
unless we find peace in our own home,
we shall not find it in the homes of others.
Let us place our trust, not in ourselves,
but in the mercy of God;
He will help us
in going from one Mansion to another,
so that we will enjoy
many more good things even in this life
than we could ever desire.

As I have written elsewhere,
when you are afflicted
by the disturbances of the devil,
recollection cannot be attained
by strenuous efforts, but comes gently,
and gradually you will be able to practice it
for longer periods at a time.
Consult people of experience about this;
you do no harm
by pursuing your necessary occupations.
Provided we do not abandon prayer,
the Lord will turn everything to our profit,
even though we find no one to teach us.

Lest any of you should think that,
since there are so many dangers,
it would be better not to enter at all
into the castle,
remember that it is absurd
to think that we can enter heaven
without first entering
into the castle of our own souls.
The door by which we enter is prayer.
We must reflect
upon the wretchedness of our own nature
and what we owe to God,

continually imploring His mercy.
The Lord himself said,
"No one will ascend to the Father, but by me";
and "He that sees me, sees the Father."

If we never think of Him,
or think what we owe Him,
or of His death for our sakes,
I do not see how we can know Him,
or do good works in His service.
What is the value of faith without good works,
works which are united
to the merits of our Lord Jesus Christ?
May His Majesty grant us
to understand how much we cost Him,
that the servant is not greater than His Lord,
and that we must work
if we are to enjoy His glory,
and for that reason we must pray,
lest we enter continually into temptation.

Third Mansions
(Two Chapters)

1 How good it is for us to be fearful of ourselves.

The man who enters the Third Mansion,
is that "blessed man who fears the Lord";
and if he continues steadfastly,
he is on the straight road to salvation,
and enjoys security of conscience.

For us Carmelites:
it is well to remember that
"Blessed is the man who fears the Lord."
We must not set store
simply by the fact
that we belong to Our Lady's Order,
and wear her habit,
or that we are cloistered
and lead lives of detachment and penance.
There are many good people
who have attained this state
of the Third Mansions;
they desire not to offend God,
they avoid venial sin, they love doing penance,
spend hours in recollection, use their time well,
and practice works of charity.

They might well go on to dwell
in the very last of the Mansions,
and they desire this;
but then we all desire it.
Words are not enough;
otherwise unless we translate them into action,
we are just like the rich young man.

We must detach ourselves
from the good works we perform,
which, after all, are trifling enough;
we must enter into ourselves,
not complaining of aridity in prayers,
which could indicate want of humility.
Let us remember with humility
how good are the lives of people
who have arrived at the Third Mansion,
and let us aim at perfection
which will be proved by works.
Not that the Lord needs our good works,
but He does need
the resoluteness of our will.

A good beginning has been made
in giving up everything for God's sake,
and if we persevere in detachment
and abandonment of everything,
we shall attain our object;
but on this condition:
we must have the humility to realize
that we are unprofitable servants,
and that our Lord is in no way obliged
to grant us His favors.

In periods of aridity, then,
we will learn to become humble,
not restless and agitated;
that's the devil's aim.
Wherever there is true humility
even if God does not grant extraordinary favors,
He will give peace and resignation to His will.
For often it is to the weakest souls
that He grants His favors
and they prefer these favors
to the fortitude which God gives
to those who have to go on in dryness of spirit.
We are all fonder of spiritual sweetness
than of crosses.

2 Aridities in prayer.

It is often disappointing
to find that some souls
who have been living
upright and carefully ordered lives
become restless and dispirited
when God gives them the cross.

They brood over their troubles,
refuse advice,
and imagine they are suffering for God,
when in reality
their troubles arise from their imperfections.
Others in this state,
conscious of their own misery,
gain by the experience,
especially in self-knowledge and humility.

There is great need
for detachment and freedom of spirit;
such things as being immersed
in buying and selling of property,
concern at loss of reputation,
worrying on account of one's imperfections,
are hardly in keeping with meditation
on the sufferings of our Lord;
not to speak of those
who are censorious about others
and want everybody
to live well-ordered lives as they do.

Those who have given up all for God
will be well able

to test their spirit of detachment
by their attitude in such situations as these;
trifling incidents arise at times
which reveal all too clearly
a want of detachment.
Religious should know
that it is not wearing the habit which counts,
but the practice of the virtues,
doing God's will, not our own.
If they find themselves lacking
at least they can try to practice humility,
which is the ointment of our wounds.
God, the Physician,
though He may delay,
will surely come to heal us
if He finds true humility.
Although these people
have a great desire for penance,
they are sure to show great discretion,
and are not at all likely to overdo it,
being eminently reasonable folk.
Reason still prevails over love;
and too often progress here
is nothing more than a snail's pace,
the road seems so difficult.

There are so many obstacles and dangers;
added to which, there is lack of courage,
the weakness of our nature,
and concern about bodily health.
The real obstacle, though,
is lack of humility,
which would make us rejoice at our weakness,
and the success of others.

Without this complete renunciation,
we find everything arduous and oppressive;
but the Lord is generous,
and sometimes grants spiritual sweetness,
which is more than we deserve.

He does not yet give
spiritual consolations, however.

Now, it may be asked,
what is the difference
between "sweetness" and "consolation"?
This will be explained later,
in the Fourth Mansions.
It is enough to say here
that there is a great difference,
and those who may receive consolations
will receive great comfort from them,
and they will humbly give thanks to God.
There should be no discouragement
if these consolations are not given;
perfection is not in these,
but in the increase of love,
and in the righteousness and truth of our actions.

What is the point,
then, of discussing interior favors
if one can attain perfection without them?
They do lead us to praise God, for His goodness
in giving them to certain souls,
and these consolations
can be a very great help
when they are from God,
in enabling the soul
to progress in love and virtue with less labor.
If, however, God should not give them,
He will show His love in some other way.
Those who are in this state
should be very diligent
in practicing ready obedience.
Let them choose a director
who is disillusioned with the things of the world,
and confide in him.
They will thus be encouraged to continue
upon hearing of the progress
others make in virtue,

and to emulate them.
It will strengthen them, too,
to bear with temptation
and not to go back to their old ways.

They are still weak,
and relatively untried by suffering,
so they need every help
to resist temptation.
We should look to our own shortcomings,
and leave other people's alone.
Those who live carefully ordered lives,
like Religious,
are too easily shocked by everything
and we might well learn important lessons
from the persons who shock us.
Outwardly, our deportment and behavior
may be better than theirs,
but this is not the only consideration,
although in itself it is good.
We must not expect everybody
to travel along the same road as ourselves,
and we should not attempt
to point out a spiritual path;
for perhaps we do not know
what it is ourselves.
We may make mistakes,
despite our good desires.
Let us do simply
what the Rule tells us:
to try to live in silence and in hope,
and the Lord will take care of His own.

Fourth Mansions
(Three Chapters)

1 The difference between sweetness and consolations. How different thought is from the understanding.

We need the help of the Holy Spirit here,
since we begin to touch on the supernatural.
It is one thing to know these things,
quite another to explain them.

In these Fourth Mansions
we come nearer to the place
where the King dwells,
in the innermost part of the castle,
that is, in the soul.
All explanations will be unintelligible
except to those
who have some experience
of what we are saying.
It seems that in order to reach this state
of the Fourth Mansions,
one normally must have lived
for a long time in the others.
However, there is no infallible rule about this
as God is not bound by rules
and gives His favors when and how He wills.
Temptations seldom trouble the soul
which is in this state,
but it is not to be regretted if they do.
It is actually a good thing,
otherwise the soul might be misled
with regard to the consolation God gives.
Temptations keep the soul on its mettle
and it is better that its absorption in God
should be interrupted at times.

Now for the distinction between
first, sweetness in prayer,
and then, spiritual consolations.

Sweetness is that which comes
from the meditations and petitions
we make ourselves,
arising from our own efforts.
We perform some virtuous work,
and feel consolation in it.
The sweetness comes from within ourselves,
though the good work is directed to God.
Spiritual consolations, however,
have their source in God,
even though they may bring us
natural joy and satisfaction.

Let us take the verse from Psalm 118,
"When you enlarged my heart."
The first kind of spiritual sweetness
does not enlarge the heart;
on the contrary,
it oppresses it in some degree.
There is on the one hand
happiness in the virtuous thing
done for God's sake,
but sorrow, too,
proceeding from our own nature.

These tears and longings
proceeding from, for example,
meditation on the Passion are good,
as they eventually lead us to God;
this happens to souls
in the first three Mansions already described,
who have to labor with the understanding
almost all the time of their prayer.
This is good,
although they should interrupt the reasoning
to praise and adore God.

If the Lord, however,
gives them the other grace of prayer,
they should not reject it
for the sake of returning to or completing
their customary meditation.
Remember, then,
if you wish to progress a long way in prayer
and reach the Mansions of your desire,
the important thing is not to think much,
but to love much;
so do whatever rouses you to love.

Some of us don't really know what love is.
It consists,
not in the extent of our happiness
but in the firmness of our determination
to please God in everything,
and to endeavor, in all possible ways,
not to offend Him,
and to pray Him ever to advance
the honor and glory of His Son
and the growth of the Catholic Church.

These are the signs of love;
do not imagine that the important thing
is never to be thinking of anything else,
and that if you become slightly distracted
all is lost.

I have sometimes been terribly oppressed
by this turmoil of thoughts
going on in the mind,
but I have come to understand
that thought, or to put it more clearly,
the imagination,
is not the same as the understanding.
I was exasperated
to see the faculties of the soul,
the intellect and the will,
united with God, while the imagination

was restless, confused, and excited,
and apparently not centered on God at all,
in a word, distracted.

We have to realize
throughout the whole experience
how much we suffer
from not knowing ourselves,
and how we worry needlessly
over what is not wrong, in fact, good.
Many people who practice prayer
go through agonies because of this,
especially if they are not instructed.
They think that
because of distractions in the imagination
they are not praying;
they become melancholic, health declines,
and they even abandon prayer altogether.
They concentrate on what is happening
in the imagination,
and its endless flights of fancy,
instead of quietly turning inward
to find God in the interior world of their soul.
It is impossible to restrain the imagination;
as well try to stop the movement of the heavens.

We think that because of these distractions
all is lost,
that we have misused the time of prayer,
when in fact at this very time
the powers of the soul
might well be wholly united to God,
with the imagination acting independently,
but not interfering with our prayer.
On the contrary,
the whole prayer is meritorious,
if the soul perseveres loyally
despite its distractions,
not abandoning the struggle,
as the devil would very much want us to do.

We should not be disturbed
or worry in the slightest about our thoughts.
They will cease
if we do not worry about them,
and if they proceed from our own weakness
we must learn to bear with them.

I do not believe
that all the scorns and trials
we have to endure in this life
can equal these interior sufferings.
We should try to be at peace,
but if the cause of the trouble is in ourselves,
the result can be unbearably painful.
Neither the will nor the understanding
ceases working in this state.

The trial may vary in intensity
according to time, season or health.
Much patience is necessary.

2 What is meant by consolations and how we obtain them. The Prayer of Quiet.

As for consolations from God,
or the Prayer of Quiet:
let us suppose there are two basins.
The water in one comes from a long distance,
and through human skill;
the other basin has been constructed
at the very source of the water
and fills without noise.
The first method represents
the spiritual sweetness produced by meditation;
we meditate, we use our intellect,
we fatigue the understanding;
the satisfaction which follows
is of our own efforts.
The second method:
the water comes direct from its source,
which is God,
and is accompanied by the greatest peace
and quietness and sweetness within ourselves.
Its source is God, it ends in ourselves;
and the whole of the outer man
enjoys this consolation and sweetness.

Its source is not in the heart,
but in a more interior part,
the center of the soul.
It causes an interior dilation
and produces ineffable blessings,
as if sweet perfumes were cast on a brazier
in the interior depths of the soul;
the fragrant light and smoke and heat
penetrate the entire soul;

and the effects extend very often even to the body.
But it is perceived
without being felt in the senses.
It is something
made of the purest gold of divine wisdom.

The genuineness of the experience
will be tested in the effects of the prayer
and actions which follow;
above all, in humility, and again, humility!

The first sign will be that you will not think
that you merit these favors and consolations
from the Lord;
and they are not to be striven after.
Following are the six reasons for this:
we should love God without any self-interest;
it would indicate lack of humility;
the true preparation is a desire
to suffer and imitate the Lord;
His majesty is not obliged to grant them;
we should be laboring in vain;
this is given only to whom God wills.

I am sure that the Lord
will not fail to grant this favor
to those who have true humility
and detachment.

3 The Prayer of Recollection.

Before experiencing the Prayer of Quiet
there is another form of prayer,
a form of recollection
which also seems to me supernatural.
It is not dependent on anything exterior;
one involuntarily closes the eyes,
and desires solitude; and without effort
there is built up a temple within
in which one can make the Prayer of Quiet.
If the senses and faculties
have wandered outside the castle,
the King, perceiving their good will,
gently calls them back to Him,
and they return to the Mansion.

When we are seeking God within ourselves,
like St. Augustine,
who, after seeking Him in many places,
found Him within himself,
it is a great help to have this favor.
Neither the understanding nor the imagination
can attain Him.
This way of seeking God is good
but this prayer (Passive Recollection)
is quite different.
These people are sometimes in the castle
before they have begun to think about God at all.
They become markedly conscious
that they are gradually retiring within themselves,
like a hedgehog, or tortoise, withdrawing into itself.
It is not a question of our will,
only God gives this

when He is pleased to do so.
I believe that He gives it
to people who are already
leaving the things of this world.

We should give God great praise
if we are granted this kind of prayer;
this prepares the soul for still greater favors.
We should be intent,
not to use our reasoning powers,
but to discover
what the Lord is working in the soul;
we never cease thinking
except when in a state of absorption.

There are three reasons
why the soul should not concern itself
about activity in this state.

First:
The person
who in this state of Recollection does most,
is he who thinks least,
and desires to do least.
We cast down our eyes in humble expectation
like poor and needy persons
before a great and rich emperor.
It is well to keep silence,
when we notice the secret signs
that He is hearing us.
There will be no harm in not striving
to labor with the understanding.
But if we are not quite sure
that the King has heard us,
we must not stay where we are like ninnies;
we should make request of the Lord,
and remember that we are in His presence,
but I cannot believe
in the efficacy of human activity
where His Majesty has reserved the action
to himself;

but we can always do for ourselves
such things as penances,
works of charity, and prayers.

Second:
All these interior activities are gentle and peaceful,
and to do anything painful
brings us harm rather than good.
Let the soul just leave itself
in the hands of God, doing His will,
disregarding its own advantage,
resigning itself entirely to His will.

Third:
The very effort the soul makes
in order to cease from thought
will perhaps awaken thought
and cause it to think a great deal.

The most important thing in God's eyes
is remembering His honor and glory,
and forgetting ourselves and our own pleasure.
How can we forget ourselves
when we are making a great effort
not even to stir?
When God wishes our understanding
to cease working,
He illumines it in another way,
in a much higher way
which may be absorption,
in which it is much better instructed
than by its own efforts.
But we must use the faculties God gave us,
not cast a spell over them,
until God sees fit
to use them for a higher purpose.

So let the soul try,
without forcing or causing turmoil,
to stop all discursive reasoning,
yet not suspend the understanding,

nor cease from all thought;
though it is well to remember
that it is in God's presence
and to recall who this God is.

If absorption is caused, well and good;
but the soul should not try
to understand what this state is;
it is only for the will to understand and enjoy it.
The will's only labor
is to utter a few loving words.

In the Prayer of Recollection, though,
even though one may not be striving
to cease from thought,
this cessation may occur,
even for a very short time.
It is unnecessary to abandon meditation
and the activities of the understanding.
In the Prayer of Quiet
the understanding may roam about
like a demented creature;
the will is so firmly fixed on God
that this disturbed condition of the understanding
causes it great distress;
but it must not take any notice of this;
it is simply to abandon itself
into the arms of divine love;
His Majesty will teach it what to do next,
and almost its whole work
is to realize its unworthiness
to receive such great good
and to occupy itself in thanksgiving.

The effects of the Prayer of Quiet are these:
there is a dilation of the soul,
as though the basin of water became larger
the more the water flowed into it;
God gradually disposes it
to retain all that He gives it.
This gentle movement

causes the soul to be less constrained
than it was before,
in matters which concern the service of God,
and this gives it much freedom.

It is not oppressed by the fear of hell,
having a firm confidence
that it is destined to have fruition of God.
Though previously afraid of penance,
it is now no longer afraid;
in fact, it thinks it can do everything;
there is no fear of trials, as before,
because it has a more lively faith;
it realizes that God will give the necessary grace
to bear them,
sometimes even to desire them.
Earthly things seem as refuse;
it withdraws from them,
and becomes more its own master.
In short, it is strengthened in all the virtues,
and will infallibly continue to increase in them
unless it turns its back on God
and commits offenses against Him.
When that happens, everything is lost,
no matter how high
a man may have climbed.

These souls are to be earnestly entreated
to exert the very greatest care
to keep themselves from occasions
of offending God.
As yet the soul is not even weaned,
but is like a child
beginning to suck the breast.
It will die if taken from its mother.
That will happen to anyone who,
having received this favor,
gives up prayer;
he will go from bad to worse.
I know souls like this who have left Him

who is yearning to give himself as a Friend
and to prove His friendship by His works.

I earnestly warn such people
not to enter upon occasions of sin,
because the devil sets greater store
by one soul in this state
than by a great number of souls
to whom the Lord does not grant these favors.
For those in this state attract others,
and can do the devil much harm,
and bring great advantage
to the Church of God.
The very fact
that the devil sees God
showing these souls special love
is sufficient to make him try
to bring about their downfall.

People in weak health should be careful
not to interpret spiritual favors they receive,
and the accompanying joy,
or "sleep," as rapture.
Such persons should take more food and sleep
and do less penance.

There may be languor in this state,
when it really comes from God,
but there will be no languor in the soul;
it is moved with great joy, being so near God.
This state, of the Prayer of Quiet,
is of short duration,
and does not overcome the body
or produce any exterior sensation.
If this should happen,
these people should tell the Superior,
and relax, with very few hours of prayer,
and more food and sleep,
until physical health returns.
If this does not suffice,

they have no contemplative vocation.
Such a person as I describe
should not be left alone very much,
or her health will be ruined.
Her vocal prayer and spirit of obedience
may bring her much benefit, however.

Fifth Mansions
(Four Chapters)

1 How the soul is united to God in prayer.

Light from heaven is needed
to describe the treasures and delights
of this Mansion.
The understanding is quite incapable
of comprehending them.

There are very few
who do not enter these Mansions.
The majority manage to get inside.
It is a great mercy of God even to reach the door.
As for us here in Carmel:
all of us who wear this holy habit
are called to prayer and contemplation.
That is the principal aim of our Order,
because we are descended
from the line of those Holy Fathers of ours
from Mount Carmel
who sought this treasure,
this precious pearl of which we speak,
in such great solitude
and such contempt for the world.

However, few of us
prepare ourselves for the Lord
to reveal it to us.
As far as externals are concerned,
we are on the right road
to attaining the essential virtues;
but we shall need to do a very great deal
before we can attain to this higher state,
and we must not be careless.
Since it is in this way possible

to enjoy heaven on earth,
let us ask the Lord to help us dig
until we find the hidden treasure,
since we have it within ourselves.

God is content
if we give all we have;
if we are to gain this treasure,
He would have us keep back nothing.
Whether it is little or much,
He would have it all for himself,
and the favors will be small or great
in accordance with what we have given.
There is no better test than this.
Here we are fast asleep
to the things of the world;
here there is no need
to devise methods for suspending thought.
Here the soul suffers
a kind of delectable death.

In the Fourth Mansion
the soul is doubtful
as to what really happened to it;
it wonders if the whole thing was imagination,
if it really came from God, or from the devil.
In this Fifth Mansion,
neither imagination, memory, nor understanding
can be an obstacle
to the blessings that are bestowed upon it.
Neither can the devil enter,
nor do any harm;
he cannot understand this secret thing.
This joy penetrates
to the very marrow of our bones.
We must not think
that God cannot grant these favors,
as some timid, half-learned men do;
those who think thus
have closed the door fast
against receiving them.

For you, a clear indication
as to whether this favor is from God is this:
God implants himself in the interior of the soul
in such a way that,
when it returns to itself,
it cannot possibly doubt
that God has been in it
and it has been in God;
if God should never grant this favor again
or for some years,
it cannot possibly doubt that it has received it.
This certainty of the soul is very real,
and it can be put there only by God.
A soul who experienced this
realized the truth of the indwelling
from this experience,
although assured otherwise
by one who was only half-learned.
This certainty has nothing to do with bodily form,
with the presence of our Lord
in the Blessed Sacrament, for example;
it has to do only with the Divinity.
It is the work of God
that we can become convinced
of something we have not seen.

Let us not perplex our understanding
in trying to understand
something that is from God;
as in the Song of Songs,
the King brought the soul
"into the cellar of wine,"
so here
we cannot enter by our own efforts,
but His Majesty must put us
right into the center of our soul,
and must enter there himself.
Our will has no part in this
and He needs no door
of the faculties of the senses to enter;
they are asleep.

2 The effects of the Prayer of Union.

L et us use a comparison to show how,
though this work is performed by the Lord,
we can do nothing to make Him grant it,
though we can do a great deal
to prepare ourselves for it.

Think of the silkworm.
First resembling a tiny seed
resting on a mulberry leaf,
it feeds on the leaf, till it is fully grown;
then it begins to spin silk from its tiny mouth
on twigs placed there for the purpose,
making for itself a tight little cocoon,
it buries itself within it;
and finally it emerges, not an ugly worm,
but a beautiful butterfly.
The wonders of God!

The silkworm is like a soul,
which takes new life,
when, through the heat
which comes from the Holy Spirit,
it makes use of the ordinary help
God gives to souls —
confessions, good books, sermons,
which helps souls in sin or temptation.
All this helps to nourish the soul,
and it grows.

When full-grown, it starts to spin its silk
and to build the house or cocoon
in which it is to die.

The house is Christ.
"Our life is hidden away with Christ in God."

His Majesty himself is our Mansion
in this prayer of union
which we ourselves spin.
When I say He will be our Mansion,
and we can construct it for ourselves
and hide ourselves within,
I do not mean
that we can add to or subtract from God;
but like these little silkworms,
we can subtract from and add to ourselves;
and God takes this tiny achievement of ours,
nothing at all,
unites it with His greatness,
and makes it of great worth;
and its reward is the Lord himself.
He unites our small trials
with the great trials that He suffered,
and makes them both into one.

So, let us hasten to spin this cocoon;
renouncing our self-love and self-will,
and our attachments to earthly things,
practicing penance, prayer,
mortification, obedience,
and other good works.
Let the silkworm die.
Then we shall see God,
and be completely hidden in His greatness.
What becomes of the silkworm?
All has been leading to this.
In this state of prayer,
it becomes a little white butterfly.
The soul cannot think
how it could merit such a blessing;
from an ugly worm to a white butterfly!
It knows that it has not merited this.
It would now gladly die

a thousand deaths for God's sake,
and has the most vehement desires
for penance, for solitude,
and that all might learn to know God.
It is greatly distressed when God is offended.

It becomes restless with desires
to do great things for God;
it places no store
on what it did previously as a "worm";
it cannot be content with crawling
when it is able to fly;
the weakness which it seemed to have before
is now turned into strength;
it is no longer bound
by ties of relationship, friendship, or poverty;
everything not of God wearies it,
and it knows
that it can find no true rest in creatures.
So the little butterfly seeks a new resting-place,
rather than earthly things;
and it is here
that its suffering really begins.
If anyone claimed that in this state
he enjoyed continual rest and joy,
I should say he had not reached it at all.
We must bear crosses in one way or another
as long as we live.

Not that those who attain this state
do not have peace;
they do, in a very high degree.
Their very trials,
coming from so noble a source,
and severe as they are,
bring peace and contentment.
But because
it is not yet perfectly conformed to God's will,
there is grief whenever it engages in prayer;
grief at how God is offended,
at how little it can do,

at the loss, and this especially,
of Christian souls.

This grief is quite different
from that which comes from meditating
on how many sins are committed,
or on how God is offended.
That grief is, as it were, achieved;
this other grief,
experienced in the Fifth Mansion,
is of quite another kind;
God impresses something of himself
on the soul,
as a seal is impressed on wax;
the soul remains soft, receptive, quiet
and consenting.

The soul shares something
of Christ's suffering in His Passion
in contemplating the sins of the world,
but also some of the joy
of doing God's will in suffering
to atone for it.

3 Another kind of union, doing the will of God. The importance of love of our neighbor.

Should the soul in this state,
with a false sense of security,
begin to lead a careless life,
and stray from the way of the Commandments,
as happens to the silkworm,
which leaves seed behind it
and then dies forever,
it may still desire others to profit,
and if it fails to profit itself, others will;
for this great favor
is not given by God in vain.
So many are called
to enjoy communion with the Lord,
and are lost, like Judas!
Our only possible safety lies in obedience,
and in never swerving from the law of God.

This Mansion always seems to be
a little obscure, and hard to describe.
Even though
the Lord withholds supernatural gifts,
we should not be without hope;
for true union can quite well be achieved,
with the favor of the Lord,
if we endeavor to attain it
by not following our own will,
but submitting it to whatever is the will of God.
I tell you,
and I say it again and again;
if you have this favor from the Lord,
of doing His will,
you need not strive

after the other delectable union
which I have described.
Conformity to the will of God
is the most valuable effect
of the union I am now describing,
and there is no attaining the heights
unless we are sure that we have the union
in which we resign our wills
to the will of God.

Happy he who has this union;
he will live peacefully
both in this life and the next.
Nothing on this earth afflicts it.

It is to be remembered
that the Lord can enrich souls in many ways
and bring them into these Mansions
by many other ways
than the shortcut described.

It is the death of the silkworm,
which is necessary, and which costs most.
Dying of our own free will
while continuing to live
is very difficult for us,
but we must not doubt
the possibility of this true union
with the will of God.
It is this union
which is so much to be desired,
the most genuine and safest.

Unfortunately there are always a few little worms
which gnaw through our virtues
(as through the ivy of Jonas),
such as self-love, self-esteem,
censoriousness (even in small things)
and lack of charity concerning our neighbors.
Thus we are far from attaining union
with the will of God.

And what is His will?
That we should be altogether perfect,
and one with Him and with the Father;
and we do not require great favors from God
in order to attain to this.
He has given us all we need
in giving us Jesus to show the way.

Do not think,
if my father or brother dies,
that I shall not grieve at the loss,
or that I shall enjoy bearing trials or illness.

The Lord really asks two things:
love of His Majesty,
and love for our neighbor.
If we have those two virtures,
we are doing His will and are united to Him.
His Majesty can give us the grace to deserve this.

The surest sign that we are keeping
these two Commandments
is that we are loving our neighbor;
we can never be sure of loving God,
but this we know quite well.
And be quite certain
that the farther advanced you are in this,
the greater will be the love you have for God.
But perfect love for our neighbor
must have its roots in God,
and in the love of God.
We should strive to know ourselves better,
and take no notice of fine plans
we make in time of prayer.
Our actions should be in harmony
with these fine plans.
This is true of all the virtues,
including humility;
the devil would run
a thousand times around hell

if he could make us believe
that we have a single virtue
which we have not in reality.

We imagine when we are at prayer
that we would be so glad
to be humbled and put to shame —
until the occasion actually arises!
The devil is simply making use of our imagination.
These resolutions are seldom in the will;
we do not sufficiently understand
the difference between faculties and imagination.

I realize how little some people understand
of the road to true union,
when I find them
so diligent about trying to discover
what kind of prayer they are experiencing,
and so completely wrapped up in their prayers
that they seem afraid to stir,
or indulge in a moment's thought,
lest they should lose in the slightest degree
the sweetness they have been feeling.
They think the whole thing consists in this
when what the Lord really desires is works.

If you see a sick woman
to whom you can give some help,
never be affected by the fear
that your devotion will suffer,
but take pity on her.
Feel her pain as if it were your own;
fast, if need be,
that she may have more food.
Then you have true union with God's will.
Also, if someone is praised in your presence,
rejoice at it,
more than if they were praising you;
if you are humble
this will come easily to you.

If we fail in this love of neighbor,
all is lost.
Always beg His Majesty
for this kind of union.
You may think that because
of devotion or consolations,
you have had some period of suspension
in the Prayer of Quiet,
but if you find you are lacking in this virtue,
you have not attained uion.
You must do violence to your own will,
so that your sisters' will
is done in everything,
even if you have to forgo your own rights
and forget your own good
for the good of others;
and this, no matter how much
you may rebel inwardly.
Think of what our Lord your Spouse
endured on the Cross.

4 The great importance of proceeding carefully.

In trying to describe this Prayer of Union,
I wish to make a comparison
with the Sacrament of Matrimony.
For the union of the soul with God
is one of love;
the union of love with love.
Everything about this union is pure,
and entirely spiritual,
very delicate and gentle,
but the Lord can make the soul
deeply conscious of this love's operation.

While this union
is not yet spiritual betrothal,
we may liken it to that of two people
who are about to be betrothed.
They discuss their suitability to each other,
and plan to meet
so that they can learn
to appreciate each other better.
So it is here;
the contract has been drawn up,
the soul is happy,
and determined to do the will of her Spouse
in every way;
His Majesty, knowing quite well that this is so,
desires that the soul
shall get to know Him better,
and that she shall be united with Him.
All this takes a very short time;
the giving and taking come to an end,
and the soul sees who this Spouse is

HICKSVILLE PUBLIC LIBRARY
169 JERUSALEM AVE.
HICKSVILLE, N.Y.

that she is to take.
This could not be understood in a thousand years
by the ordinary use
of the senses and the faculties.
After this one visit,
the Spouse leaves the soul worthier
to join hands with Him;
the soul is inflamed with love for Him.
If, however, through neglect
the heart is set
on anything other than herself
everything is lost.

So, every effort should be made
to withdraw from occasions of sin;
for in this state,
the betrothal not yet having been made,
the soul is not strong enough.
The devil will use every means
to prevent the betrothal.
Afterwards, when he sees the soul
completely surrendered to the Spouse,
he is afraid, knowing he will be the loser.

I know persons
of a very high degree of spirituality
whom the devil, with great subtlety,
has won back to himself.
He will marshall all the powers of hell,
for to win one soul like this
is to win a whole multitude.
Think of the harm
done to the devil's cause by the Saints,
like St. Ursula, St. Dominic, St. Francis,
St. Ignatius.
Remember that all they did
was not to frustrate the divine betrothal
through their own fault.
There are so few
who wish to receive the Lord's favors,

that it is still necessary
that we should wish to receive them.

You might well ask two questions here.
First,
how can a soul be completely deceived
when it is so united with the will of God,
and since it never desires to do its own will?
Second,
by what avenues can the devil enter,
if the soul is so completely withdrawn
from the world,
and frequently receives the Sacraments?

In answer to the first question:
the devil, in trivial ways,
undermines the soul's good intentions,
and convinces it
that certain practices are not wrong;
self-love increases,
the understanding is darkened,
the will is weakened,
and in one way or another
the soul withdraws from the love of God,
and indulges its own wishes.

And this also answers the second question.
The Lord permits this
so that He can observe
the behavior of this soul
whom He wants to shine forth
as a light before others;
it is better that it should be so at the outset,
than when it has done many souls harm.

So we must constantly ask God in our prayers
to keep us in His hand,
remembering always that if He leaves us,
we shall be down in the depths at once;
but we must have confidence in ourselves.

With special care and attention,
we must watch the progress
we make in the virtues,
especially in our love for each other
and in the desire to be thought least of,
and in ordinary things.

Do not imagine
that the Lord easily allows a soul like this
to go quickly out of His hand,
so that the devil can recapture it
without much labor.
On the contrary,
He gives it a thousand interior warnings
so that it cannot fail to perceive the danger.
So we must strive at all times to advance;
failure to advance would be a very bad sign.

Now that we intend to describe
the Sixth Mansions,
it will be apparent
how slight is the effort we really make
and the service we render God.
It would ill become us to lie down
and go to sleep again.

Sixth Mansions
(Eleven Chapters)

1 The soul which is granted great favors must endure great trials.

The help of the Holy Spirit is needed here;
the soul, wounded with love, desires solitude,
and tries to renounce everything
which would disturb it.
This is in order to recover
the "sight" of the Beloved
(not sight in the ordinary sense,
even of the imagination).
The soul now greatly desires perfect union,
which is called betrothal,
but the Spouse disregards her yearnings.
Instead, He allows the soul
to be afflicted with the severest trials.
If the soul realized beforehand
the extent of the suffering involved,
it is doubtful
if she would have the strength to go on.
Her motives are misunderstood,
and this is a great trial;
she does her best to correspond with grace,
and people mock her for "trying to be holy";
she is "obviously deluded";
"the devil's in it," and so on.

This kind of trial
can go right on throughout one's life.
Others praise her holiness,
and this becomes intolerable,
especially in the beginning.
Gradually less notice is taken of what people say;

the soul realizes
that people are as ready to praise as to blame;
and is acutely aware
that any good in her comes from God;
further, she realizes that this praise
can really do her no harm.
Neither does she fear censure;
rather, she tends to be grateful to her critics.
The Lord may also send
grievous pains and infirmities of body.

These physical trials, however,
are nothing compared to interior trials.
The first of these
comes from having a scrupulous confessor,
who is afraid that everything unusual
proceeds either from the devil or from melancholy.
So he condemns the soul
and she is greatly upset,
thinking herself perhaps deceived
and more conscious than ever
of her past sinfulness.
She becomes more and more fearful,
especially when periods of aridity follow.
She then wonders
if she has deceived her confessor,
and our Lord allows the devil
to tempt her into thinking
that she is cast off by God.
Interior sufferings follow,
so terrible as to be intolerable.
No consolation is possible in this state,
and it can be compared only
to the sufferings of hell.

The thing to do is simply to wait
for the mercy of God,
who suddenly lifts the burden unexpectedly.
All becomes well again;
the soul regains its happiness

and realizes clearly its own helplessness,
and the need of God in such trials.

If these trials described above
should continue for a long time,
there seems only one thing to do.
When mental prayer seems impossible,
solitude a torture,
as is also the company of other people,
she becomes very despondent,
and is unable to explain her state to anyone.
The best medicine of all
is to occupy oneself with external affairs
and works of charity,
and to hope in the mercy of God.

Thus at least it will become endurable.
It will be remembered
that the devil cannot cause this kind of interior trial,
as he has no power
over the interior faculties of the soul,
the intellect and the will.

2 How we deal with the way in which the Spouse awakens the soul.

He fills it with fervent desires,
but so delicately
that the soul does not understand them;
only those who have experienced them
will understand,
so delicate and subtle are they.
The consolations experienced here
are very different from those already described.
For often God awakens the soul,
as by a thunderclap,
when it is quite unprepared
and not even thinking of Him.
It is a delectable wound;
the soul's reaction is to tremble, even complain;
yet, recognizing the wound
as a precious experience,
and not wishing to be healed,
it is grief-stricken,
because God does not fully reveal himself.
There is distress along with great joy;
a joy much more satisfying
than that of the Prayer of Quiet.
The Beloved's call is very clear;
the soul has no doubt of it, it is so penetrating.
The senses, the imagination,
and the other faculties seem to be at rest,
not daring to stir.

The soul has a clear consciousness
of God's presence.
Yet the distress it feels is terrible,
penetrating, like an arrow

which, piercing to the very entrails,
is withdrawn.
Perhaps the best comparison
is that of a spark from the divine fire
which enkindles the soul.
The spark, while burning,
never really enkindles or sets the soul on fire;
it dies, leaving a deep yearning
to suffer again the loving pain.

There is no doubt
that this comes from the Lord;
there is no deception or fancy,
nor can it proceed from melancholy,
or the devil.
It is perfectly clear that its source is the Lord.
There need be no fear of deception
in the soul who has received this; rather,
he should be full of gratitude to God.

The reasons for the security one feels
about this situation are these.
First, pain which is caused by the devil
is never accompanied by peace,
but is restless and combative.
Second, the advantages to the soul
are so great, namely,
determination in suffering trials,
and a firm resolution
to withdraw from the pleasures of the world.

When this movement is genuine
the soul has no doubt of it whatever;
indeed doubt as to whether
it has experienced this
would be a sure sign that it is not genuine.
There will be no fears about this kind of prayer.

The Lord has other methods, too,
of awakening the soul.

Quite unexpectedly, during vocal prayer,
while not thinking of interior things,
it seems to catch fire,
as though a fragrance diffused itself powerfully
through all the senses;
not a real fragrance, of course,
but indicating the presence of the Spouse.
There follows a delectable desire to enjoy Him
and the soul makes many acts of praise
to the Lord.
These desires cause no pain.

3 The way in which God speaks to the soul.

Another way in which God awakens the soul
is by locutions.
Some of these come from without;
some from the innermost depths of the soul;
some from its highest part;
others seem to be uttered by a human voice.

Sometimes this may be a fancy,
especially in melancholy persons.
These should be treated as sick,
and it is better to humor them,
than to reprimand or contradict them.
Both infirm and healthy souls
should have cause for misgivings
about these things
until it is clearly discerned whence they come.
It is always better to dispense with them at first,
thus putting them to the proof.
Distress or disquiet is to be avoided.
Locutions may come from God,
from one's own imagination,
or from the devil.

The first sign that a locution comes from God
is the sense of power and authority
the locution bears with it,
and the sense of confidence and peace
that follows it.
Such a word as "It is I, fear not,"
in distress of soul,
brings marvelous comfort,
when all other comfort fails.

The second sign is tranquillity in the soul,
a peaceful and devout recollection,
and a desire to sing the praises of God.

The third sign is this:
The words do not vanish from the memory
for a long time; perhaps, never.
If they concern the future,
containing some prediction,
the soul has the utter certainty
that it will come true,
no matter how ridiculous
this may seem to be at the time,
and no matter what suffering may be caused
by the scoffing of others, including the confessor,
who may describe these locutions
as pure nonsense.

The spark of certainty always remains
and the joy
in eventually seeing the Lord's word fulfilled
is great indeed.

If the locutions come from the imagination,
none of these signs occurs,
nor any certainty or peace,
nor interior consolation.
Some persons
who are carried out of themselves
in the Prayer of Quiet
can have these "locutions" in the imagination
at this time,
and should not be deceived into thinking
that they come from God.
The devil's locutions are more to be feared
than those coming from the imagination;
but if the signs already described are present,
one may be confident they are from God.
Not that one should act on this
without the advice of one's confessor,
in matters involving oneself, or a third person,

even though from the signs
one becomes certain they are from God.
This is God's will,
and following one's opinion in these matters
is dangerous.

Another way in which the Lord
speaks to the soul
is by an intellectual vision.
The way in which the soul understands
the words spoken by the Lord
is that the soul is convinced,
also from the good effects that follow,
that the devil can have no part in the matter.

The first reason lies
in the clarity of the genuine locution;
every syllable is heard and understood;
in those locutions
created fancifully by the imagination
the voice and word will be indistinct
like something heard in a half-dream.

The second reason is
that often the soul has not been thinking
of what it hears;
the voice comes unexpectedly
and refers to things
which one never thought would happen;
they could not possibly have been invented.

The third reason:
In genuine locutions
the soul seems to be hearing something;
in those of the imagination
it is as if someone were composing bit by bit
what the soul wishes to hear.

The fourth reason:
The words themselves;

one single word contains a whole world
of meaning.

The fifth reason:
Much more will be understood
beyond that which the words convey.
Some are unable to understand
whether the locutions are genuine or not;
while the devil will be able to speak clearly,
the effects will be different —
only restlessness and turmoil,
instead of peace and light.
No harm can come to the soul
as long as it refrains from action,
whatever the locutions may say.

If gifts and favors come from the Lord,
the soul should take note of the fact
that the greater the favor,
the less it will esteem itself,
the more keenly it will remember its sins,
and the more forgetful it will be of its own interest.
It will seek nothing
but the honor and glory of God,
and it will be in great fear
of departing in the least from the will of God.
If these dispositions result,
there need be no fear of deception by the devil.

To those who suggest
that when these occur
one's attention should be turned elsewhere,
I reply that this is impossible;
if they are from God
the Spirit himself inhibits all thought
and compels attention.

4 Occasions when God suspends the soul in rapture, ecstasy or trance.

Because our nature is timid and lowly,
great courage is necessary
to achieve union with so great a Lord;
and the Lord, to encourage us,
and knowing our weakness,
continues to grant favors.
Unless God granted us the strength
it would be impossible to go on;
so God bestows raptures,
and it is of these that we shall now speak.

One kind of rapture is this:
though not actually engaged in prayer,
the soul is struck by some word,
which it either remembers
or hears spoken by God.
It seems to catch fire and spring to new life;
its sins are cleansed,
and God unites it with himself
in a way none can understand,
save the soul and God.
The soul is incapable
of speaking of it afterwards,
but at the time
is not deprived of the interior senses.
The soul has never before been so awake
to the things of God,
or had such light and knowledge of God;
even though both senses and faculties
were completely absorbed.

Also, if the soul has intellectual visions,
they cannot be described,

except perhaps after the soul
has regained its senses;
the profit to the soul is so great
that it cannot be exaggerated.
The favors are imprinted in the soul,
in its very depths,
and they are never forgotten.
Just as marvelous things
were revealed to Moses
when he saw the burning bush,
and these things gave him courage
to do what he did for the people of Israel,
and Jacob learned great secrets
in the vision of the ladder
ascending to the heavens,
so the soul is able to apprehend
supernatural truths
according to the pleasure of God revealing them,
without remembering in detail
all the things it has seen.

Remember, we are speaking of intellectual,
not imaginary visions,
and it is my belief
that if the soul does not understand
the secrets God is revealing,
they are not raptures at all,
but rather some form of absorption
proceeding from weakness.
If the soul is enraptured,
you can be sure
that God is taking the soul entirely to himself.
When He means to enrapture a soul,
it loses its power of breathing,
and cannot speak,
although the other senses
may remain active a little longer.
At other times,
it loses all the powers at once,
and the soul seems
to have departed from the body

and it seems not to breathe.
All this lasts only a short time,
but may be repeated again and again.
Complete ecstasy lasts only a short time.
This ecstasy, however,
has the effect of leaving the will
so completely absorbed,
and the understanding
so completely transported,
that the soul
seems incapable of grasping anything
that does not awaken the will to love.

When it comes to itself,
the soul is filled with ardent desires
to be used for God
in any way He pleases;
gladly it would give God a thousand lives,
and would wish every tongue on earth
to praise Him;
it has tremendous desires to do penances
and complains to God that it does not suffer.
With the aid of God, suffering becomes easy.

The soul suffers embarrassment from others
who notice this enraptured state;
this could be lack of humility,
but the Lord can bring comfort and reassurance;
it is certain that from now on
He intends to have the soul for himself,
whatever attacks may be made against her.
Henceforth the Lord will protect her
from the whole world
and indeed from hell itself.

5 How God exalts the soul through flights of the spirit.

We now deal with another kind of rapture,
    which we will call flight of the spirit;
substantially the same as that just described.
It is felt differently within the soul.
This transport of the spirit
takes place so rapidly
that the soul is at first filled with fear,
and great courage is necessary to bear it,
together with faith and confidence
and great resignation.
Resistance is impossible,
and the effort makes matters worse.
It is like a great flood tide
released by God to sweep the soul on high;
just as a little ship
is borne aloft on a giant wave
and neither pilot nor crew
can do anything to prevent it.
The result of this action of God
is that the soul realizes its own foolishness,
and the worthlessness of its own good actions.

It remembers only its sins and imperfections
and throws itself more readily
on the mercy of God.

The soul really seems to have left the body
in this flight of the spirit,
but it is clear,
despite appearances to the contrary,
that the person is not dead.
He feels as if he has been in another world,

very different from this one,
and in a single instant
he is taught so many things at once
that he cannot fit them all
into his imagination and thought.

This imaginary vision is seen with the eyes
of the soul
much more clearly
than we can see with the eyes of the body;
revelations are communicated without words,
and if, for example,
he sees any of the Saints,
he immediately recognizes them.
Some admirable kind of knowledge
reveals these things,
and when the soul returns to itself,
it finds it has reaped great advantages,
and all earthly things seem like dirt to it.
Just to go on living seems a great affliction.

The soul reaps three distinct benefits,
which shows clearly that this grace is genuine
and not from the devil:
first, knowledge of the greatness of God;
second, self-knowledge and humility,
which comes from the realization
that it could even have offended
one who is the Creator of such greatness;
third, a supreme contempt for earthly things,
save those which can be employed
in the service of so great a God.

6 How this prayer will be known as genuine.

The soul is now so anxious
to have complete fruition
of the Giver of these great favors
that life becomes sheer,
though delectable, torture.
She has the keenest longings for death,
and frequently, tearfully,
begs God to take her out of exile.
She can find no lasting repose;
everything connected with God's love
causes raptures which occur continually
and cannot be avoided, even in public.
There is much persecution and suffering,
especially from confessors.
She experiences on the one hand
great interior security
especially when alone with God,
but on the other hand
she is afraid of deception by the devil.
She is distressed
when her confessor blames her
for these raptures,
but cares not at all for other people's criticism.

She realizes that this road is,
in their opinion, very dangerous,
begs their prayers and asks that God
will lead her by another, safer road.
Yet, so much has she gained
from following this way, that,
try as she may,

she feels unable to desire any other.
She is distressed
over the impotence of her will
and over her venial sins,
as God gives her the keenest desire
not to displease Him in any way,
however slight.
She experiences contrary desires —
to retire into a desert,
or to plunge right into the heart of the world,
if by so doing God can be praised more.

These desires are not fleeting, but permanent,
but with regard to the great desires
the soul may have to see our Lord,
they should be put aside, not encouraged.
With regard to shedding tears,
it could be helpful,
but that is not the important thing;
we should work hard, practice the virtues,
and make no effort to induce tears.

Sometimes
our Lord bestows on the soul in this state
a jubilation and a strange kind of prayer
whose nature I cannot ascertain;
in this state the soul cannot remain silent,
like St. Francis,
who could not but praise the Lord aloud.
It is an entirely supernatural thing;
we cannot acquire it.
The soul is so forgetful of itself, and of everything,
that it is conscious of nothing
except the joy of praising God.

7 The importance of keeping in mind the sacred Humanity of Christ.

Lest some should think
that these souls will now be so sure of themselves
that they need not fear or weep for their sins,
let it be remembered
that the more they receive from God,
the greater grows their sorrow for sin.
The soul remembers how ungrateful
it has been to Him to whom it owes so much,
and its sins are always in its memory.
With regard to fear of hell,
these souls have none.
Their only reason
for not desiring to stay in purgatory
is that they will not be with God there.

The soul should on no account think it is secure,
or forget the miserable state it was once in.
We shall always have failures in this mortal life,
no matter how virtuous we may seem to be;
we know our sins are forgiven,
yet the thought of the goodness God shows,
and the favors He gives despite our sins,
causes much distress,
as must have been the case
with St. Peter and St. Mary Magdalene.

It would be quite wrong to imagine
that in this state
one will not meditate
on the most sacred Humanity
of our Lord Jesus Christ.
This is very important.

There are some souls who think
that they cannot dwell on the Passion,
still less meditate on the most sacred Virgin
and the lives of the Saints.
This is inconceivable;
we are not disembodied spirits
and we need to cultivate,
think upon, and seek the companionship
of those who,
though living on earth like ourselves,
have accomplished great deeds for God;
and above all we must not withdraw
from our greatest help and blessing,
the most sacred Humanity
of our Lord Jesus Christ.

If anyone should fail to do this,
she will not enter the last two Mansions;
if she loses her guide, the good Jesus,
she will be unable to find her way.
He is the "Way," the "Light,"
and no one can come to the Father
except by Him.

Those people who fondly imagine that,
having received this gift of contemplation,
they will remain in possession of it forever,
are mistaken.
It is true
that the soul has less aptitude
for laboring with the understanding,
and the soul readily seeks Him
in the will alone;
but the will
must not entirely set aside the intellect,
and it is impossible to do so,
especially before the soul has reached
these last Mansions.
The aid of the understanding
is often needed to enkindle the will.
We cannot expect miracles,

and the will,
even though desirous of loving alone,
needs to be enkindled.
When there is a state of aridity,
it is good for us to realize
our weakness and our wickedness,
and we must help ourselves
by using the understanding
when in this state of dryness,
which, I think,
will continue to occur until we die.

It is true that anyone
in the Seventh Mansion rarely, if ever,
needs to engage in this activity;
there we never cease to walk
in the company of Christ our Lord.
Until we arrive at this state
we must do everything possible
to help ourselves,
and not foolishly lose time
waiting to receive favors.
We have to meditate
on the life and death of Christ,
and strive to keep the Commandments
and counsels; and remember
that the Lord may delay
the repetition of His gifts
for a very long time, even years.
That is His concern, not ours.

Here a distinction should be made
between reasoning with the understanding
and representing truths to the understanding.
The first is what I call meditation,
and since it means meditating in detail
on the mysteries
of Christ's life and death, and Passion,
it is difficult
for those who have been given the favors
spoken about above to do this.

But for them,
there is no difficulty
about apprehending these mysteries
with the understanding;
so that both the memory and understanding
work together to consider,
with a simple regard,
who He is, how ungrateful we have been;
the mystery itself of God's goodness
in one consideration alone
of Christ's Passion,
or any other representation
of a scene from His life.
The soul should do this,
since no sublime method of prayer
will be an obstacle to this.
It must not labor hard
at meditation of the first kind,
that is true; in any case,
that kind of labor is impossible
for a person
who has attained great heights in prayer;
but the second way,
of representing the mysteries,
is extremely beneficial.
The Lord will suspend the faculties then
if He wishes.

Some souls,
at the beginning of the spiritual life
or even if they have reached
the state of the Prayer of Quiet,
think that
they should enjoy the gifts and favors
of this state all the time.
My advice to them
is to become less absorbed in favors.
Rather, look at Christ;
reflect how He, and the Apostles and Saints,
bore the many trials of life,
so that we, too,

may bear them perfectly.
We must not forsake Jesus
and His most holy Mother.
He is pleased
when we grieve for His afflictions,
and if anybody were to tell me
that she enjoyed consolations in prayer
so continuously
that she could never meditate
I should consider it suspicious.
Keep on meditating, then,
and make every effort
to avoid this absorption.

As for the benefits of meditating
on the sacred Humanity,
His most sacred Mother's love
was so perfect,
she was firm in the faith
and she knew He was both God and man,
but His bodily presence
in the sacred Humanity was a help,
by no means a hindrance, to her.

8 How God communicates with the soul through intellectual visions.

Let us consider that,
when His Majesty so wills,
we cannot do otherwise
than walk with Him all the time.
The farther a soul progresses,
the closer becomes its companionship
with the good Jesus.
It may happen that the soul,
when least expecting it,
is conscious that Jesus Christ our Lord
is near to it,
though it cannot see Him,
either with the eyes of the body
or of the soul.
This is called an intellectual vision.
The soul has certainty
that it is really Jesus Christ our Lord
but has misgivings about it,
even though the effects produced in the soul
are so remarkable.

This vision, unlike an imaginary one,
which lasts a very short time,
lasts many days,
sometimes for more than a year.

She sees nothing in the ordinary way,
face or hands, or anything else;
she simply feels certain it is Christ,
and has no doubt
about the genuineness of the vision.
Especially as the Lord may say

some consoling words like,
"Be not afraid: it is I."
She then realizes that it is a great help
to be thus continually thinking of God,
trying always to please Him,
and feeling that He is always looking at her.
Not that she can hear Him speak
whenever she wishes.
She is conscious of Him
walking at her right hand,
not through the senses,
but in a much more subtle way.
The effect is of such peace
and constant desire to please God
that it could not come from the devil.
It brings also great confusion
and humility, and the knowledge
of God's constant companionship
begets a most tender love
toward His Majesty,
yearnings to give oneself wholly
to His service,
and great purity of conscience;
for the Presence
which the soul has at its side
makes it sensitive to everything.
Though other favors so far described
may be greater than this,
this brings a special knowledge of God,
and the certainty of His presence
which otherwise may easily be lost sight of.
A vivid and conscious love of God results,
filling the soul with thanksgiving
for a treasure which it would not exchange
for any earthly joy.
Sometimes the presence is of a Saint,
or of the Blessed Mother.

In this situation
it is desirable to seek out
the advice of a confessor

who is both spiritual and learned,
not, however,
to indulge in endless consultations,
but to report the matter calmly
and not to allow it
to be noised abroad.
No sister should think
she is better than the rest,
simply because of these favors.
Sometimes it is the weakest
God leads by this road,
and we must base our judgment of a person
on her practice of the virtues.

The saintliest is she
who serves our Lord
with the greatest mortification
and humility and purity of conscience.
At the Judgment we shall know
how different God's judgments are from ours.

9 How the Lord communicates himself through imaginary visions. We should not desire to walk in this way.

It is said
that the devil interferes more frequently
in imaginary visions,
with which we shall now deal.

Suppose we carried about with us
a gold reliquary
in which there was hidden a precious stone;
we know the stone is there,
though we have never seen it,
and dare not open the reliquary.
It has cured us of certain illnesses,
and only the owner of the jewel
knows how to open the reliquary.
Let us suppose that one day
we suddenly open it.
Imagine the great pleasure
we would derive from seeing its brilliance,
and afterwards recalling its great beauty;
seeing it engraves the memory of it
deeply in the mind.

That is what happens
when the Lord wishes to give
a clear revelation of His sacred Humanity,
either as He was when He lived on earth,
or after His Resurrection.
This revelation is so sudden
that it is like a flash of lightning,
but so deeply is it engraven
on the imagination
that it will not be erased in this life.
I use the word "image,"

but it is not as in a painting,
it is really alive,
and sometimes even speaks,
revealing great, secret things.

The soul
cannot gaze on such brilliance for long;
not that its interior sight is hurt
as the natural eye is by the sun,
but that the soul is enraptured
when the vision passes.
Its brilliance is like that of an infused light
or a sun covered with a material
of the transparency of diamond.
The soul is filled with a great terror
at so magnificent a sight;
it knows
that it is the Lord of heaven and earth,
and this without being told.
It realizes that,
if such terror results in the soul
when the Lord comes,
in such a loving, friendly fashion,
how terrible it must be on Judgment Day
to hear, "Depart, accursed of my Father!"

So this soul never fears hell
so much as the thought
of seeing the wrath in the eyes of one
so tender and loving.
When the soul is able to remain
for a long time
looking upon the Lord,
I do not think it can be a vision at all.
Perhaps it is a striking idea
creating a picture in the imagination,
but it is a dead thing
compared to what I am describing.

There are some persons,
and a great many, indeed,

whose imaginations and intellects are so lively,
that they think
they actually see everything in their mind.
This produces no good effect
and no attention should be paid
to such a thing if it occurs.

The genuine vision I am describing
takes place quite unexpectedly,
like St. Paul's vision on the way to Damascus,
when out of a sudden, violent fear
there came a great calm,
and the complete certainty
that the favor came from God.
This is so,
even though the confessor
should insinuate the fear of being mistaken,
and the devil should try to confuse it;
but the soul never loses its feeling of certainty.

It is not surprising
that confessors should have doubts,
and they must proceed cautiously;
but an experienced confessor,
especially if he has had personal experience
of what I am describing,
will readily recognize
by the effects in the soul
whether the vision is genuine or not.

It is essential to be frank with one's confessor
about these matters;
God is very anxious
that you speak candidly and clearly
in relating them,
and acquaint him with all your thoughts,
still more with your actions, however trivial.

If this is done,
there need be no disturbance of mind,
even if these things be not from God;

they will do no harm if there is humility,
and a good conscience.
Even if the devil
should cause the image of the Lord
which you see,
God can draw good out of it,
and you may even be quickened
in your devotion as a result of it.

If you should learn
that anyone is being granted these graces,
you must never beseech or desire the Lord
to lead you along this road.

Here are my reasons.
First:
It would show lack of humility.
Self-knowledge is always God's gift
to anyone receiving these favors;
how could they be desired?
Second:
Such a person
is certain to be deceived by the devil.
Third:
The imagination goes to work,
and this person simply imagines
what she desires to see.
Fourth:
It would show presumption
in choosing one's own path to God.
Fifth:
The trials accompanying this way are heavy;
could they be borne?
Sixth:
The very thing from which gain is expected
may bring loss.

No, we must do God's will, not our own;
remember that we merit no more glory
for having received these favors,
rather, we incur heavy obligations.

Many saintly people have never known
these favors,
while others who receive them are not saintly.
It is true that to have these favors
must be the greatest help
toward attaining a high degree
of perfection in the virtues;
but anyone who has attained the virtues
at the cost of his own toil
has earned more merit.
A soul truly on fire with love
does not serve the Lord for pay;
and the nature of love
is that it invariably finds expression
in work of a thousand kinds.

10 Of other favors, and the great profit from them.

All this is to help souls to understand
that if they should see a vision,
they will not be disturbed or distressed.
This only pleases the devil.

It may happen that the soul is at prayer
and the Lord causes suspension of its senses;
secret things are communicated to the soul,
and it realizes how all things are seen in God,
and how within himself
He contains them all.
This lasts but a moment,
but is highly profitable.
It is an intellectual vision,
in which we clearly realize
that in committing sin
we do so within God himself.
We realize the great mercy of God
in not casting us straight into hell,
and resolve to endure everything
and love those who do us wrong.
If God forgives so, should we not, too?

God may also very suddenly reveal
a truth that is in himself alone,
and we realize
how little we understand of Sovereign Truth
here on earth.
We should always walk in this truth,
and seek after truth in everything.
I suddenly realized once
why God loves the virtue of humility so much;

it is because He is Sovereign Truth
and to be humble is to walk in truth.
Anyone who does not realize
that we have no good in ourselves
is walking in falsehood.

11 The desires felt by the soul to enjoy God; the profit from this favor.

The more the soul learns
about the greatness and goodness of God,
the more her desire increases,
and the more her love continues to grow.
Her desires become so great
as to cause her great distress.

While the soul is in this state
of interior yearning and distress,
it often happens
that a mere thought of some kind
deals, as it were, a blow,
or wounds it with a fiery arrow
in its most intimate depths.
The faculties are enchained,
with no freedom of action.
God gives a lively knowledge of himself,
with keen distress because of His absence;
the soul cries out aloud,
suffering as it does, not in the body,
but deep within the soul — a suffering
which resembles that of purgatory.
The soul thinks it is dying;
the limbs are disjointed
and the pulse rate feeble.

All this lasts a very short time,
but if the flame were a little stronger,
the soul's desires to be with God
would surely be fulfilled.
There is no bodily pain;
in fact, the body seems to gain strength
from the experience.

Up to this,
the soul seemed perfectly resigned
to the will of God;
now she can think of nothing
but the cause of her suffering.
Why, she asks,
should she continue to live?
She experiences a strange solitude,
and no creature on the whole earth
can be a companion to her,
or, for that matter, in heaven, either.
The great thirst she feels
can be quenched by God alone.
Nevertheless the soul feels
the pain to be so precious
that she fully realizes
she could never deserve it,
and suffers it very gladly;
indeed she would suffer it all her life long.

Contrast this
with the suffering of the souls in hell.
They are not resigned,
nor have they contentment in their suffering,
like this soul.
The suffering of the soul
is so much more grievous and terrible
than the suffering of the body.
The soul in this state,
receiving these favors from God,
remains thus for only a short time,
at most, three or four hours.
The pain is more than she can bear,
and she yearns to die;
her soul seems on the point of leaving the body.
She is really afraid,
and would like her distress to be alleviated
lest she should die;
a fear that comes from her natural weakness.
Only the Lord can relieve her distress,
and this in fact He does,

granting her a deep rapture
in which He comforts and strengthens her
so that she can wish to live
for as long as He wills.

The soul at last loses its fear
of any trials which may befall it;
it sees that no worldly things
were of any avail in its torment;
it becomes much more detached
from creatures, as it knows
that it can be comforted only by the Creator.
So, courage is necessary
if we are to travel by this road;
if you ask the Lord for these things,
be ready to answer the question,
"Can you drink the chalice?"
We should reply, "We can";
for the Lord gives the strength
to those who have need of it,
and defends them
if they are persecuted and spoken ill of,
as He did for the Magdalen.
And in the end,
He more than repays them for everything at once,
as we shall see.

Seventh Mansions
(Four Chapters)

1 The great favors in this Mansion; the difference between soul and spirit.

Before consummating the spiritual marriage,
our Lord brings the soul,
which He has now taken spiritually as His bride,
into this Mansion of His, the seventh.
He needs an abiding-place in the soul
as He has in heaven.
It becomes a second heaven.
In this Mansion,
everything is different from previous Mansions.
In those the soul was affected
only in its highest part;
the Lord united it with himself,
but He made it blind and dumb
to what was happening,
except for its vivid realization
of the nearness of God.
The faculties are all lost.

Now the scales are removed from its eyes;
it sees and understands something
of the favor given to it.
It is brought into this Mansion
by an intellectual vision,
in which the Most Holy Trinity reveals itself,
in all three Persons.
The spirit is enkindled and illumined
by a cloud of great brightness.
It sees these three Persons, individually,
yet, by a wonderful kind of knowledge,
it realizes that most certainly
all these three Persons

are one substance and one power
and one knowledge
and one God alone.
What we hold by faith,
the soul grasps by sight.
Nothing is seen by the eyes
either of the body or the soul;
it is not an imaginary vision,
but an intellectual vision.

All three Persons communicate themselves
to the soul, and speak to it,
explaining the words of the Gospel,
that "He and the Father and the Holy Spirit
will come to dwell
with the soul which loves Him
and keeps His commandments" (John 14:23).
What a difference between hearing these words,
and believing them,
and realizing how true they are!
The soul sees that these three Persons
are in the interior of her soul,
in the most interior place.
She feels this divine companionship
within herself.

Not that she is unable to fix her mind on nothing else.
On the contrary,
she is in complete possession of her senses
and is more alert than before
in all that pertains to the service of God.
When not otherwise occupied,
she remains in this happy companionship.
She works more carefully than ever,
so as not to displease God,
but remains confident
that He will continue to give her
the most certain assurance of His presence.

This presence is not realized always
so fully or clearly

as when it first comes,
or as happens on certain occasions;
otherwise the soul could not go on living,
or think of anything else.
But it always has the awareness
of this companionship.

She is greatly assisted
to go onward to perfection
and to lose the fear
she had in the previous states;
she finds herself better in every way,
and the essential part of the soul
never moves from that dwelling place,
however numerous her trials and worries.
She seems to feel divided within herself,
but this is only apparent,
and is explained
by the division of soul and spirit,
which are different, though one.
Sometimes their operations seem to differ
just as the respective joys
which the Lord gives to the one and the other.
The soul is different from the faculties, too;
they are not one and the same.
All will be revealed about these things
in the life to come.

2 The difference between spiritual union and spiritual marriage.

The divine and spiritual marriage
of which we are about to speak
cannot be fulfilled perfectly in this life,
since it could be lost
if we withdraw ourselves from God.
When granting this favor for the first time,
our Lord reveals himself
through an imaginary vision
of His most sacred Humanity,
so that we may clearly understand
what is taking place.

To this person
the Lord revealed himself one day
after Holy Communion
in great beauty and splendor,
as He did after the Resurrection,
and told her that it was time
she took upon her His affairs
as if they were her own
and that He would take her affairs upon himself.
You might think
that there was nothing new in this,
but in fact it was so different
that it left her quite confused and dismayed,
because of the force of the vision,
the words He spoke, and because
she had never before had visions like this
in the interior of the soul.

It must be understood
that there is the greatest difference

between all other visions mentioned before
and those that belong to this Mansion,
and the same difference
between spiritual bethrothal
and spiritual marriage
as between two betrothed persons
and two who are united
so that they cannot be separated any more.

Of course it is to be remembered
that in neither case
has the betrothal or union
anything to do with the body;
in the spiritual marriage
the union takes place
in the deepest center of the soul
which must be where God dwells.
There is no need of a door
by which to enter it,
as in the other Mansions;
all that has taken place up to this
has come through the medium
of the senses and faculties;
and this applies to the appearances
of the Humanity of our Lord, too.

In the spiritual marriage all is different;
the Lord appears in the center of the soul,
not in an imaginary, but an intellectual vision,
subtler than that already mentioned,
just as He, the Lord,
appeared to the Apostles
without entering the door,
as in John 20:19-21.
In an instantaneous communication
of God to the soul, secret and sublime,
the Lord is pleased to reveal to the soul
the glory that is in heaven,
to its intense delight.
The spirit of the soul
is made one spirit with God

in a union of two
who cannot be separated from each other.

In the spiritual betrothal,
there is this difference,
that the two persons are frequently separated,
and afterwards the soul
is deprived of this companionship.
In this favor, spiritual marriage,
the soul remains all the time
in the center with its God.
In union of betrothal it is as though
two wax candles are united,
becoming one,
but they can be separated again.

In spiritual marriage,
it is like rain falling from heaven
into a river or spring,
or a tiny streamlet entering the sea;
there is no way of separating the two waters,
once united.
Or again,
it is like light from two windows
entering a room and becoming one.

As St. Paul says,
"He who is joined to God
becomes one spirit with Him,"
and "For me to live is Christ, to die, again";
the little butterfly of the previous Mansions
now dies,
because Christ is now her life.
As time passes,
the soul clearly understands
that it is endowed with life by God.
Certain delectable words it utters
produce this feeling,
as though streams of milk
were flowing from the divine breasts
to sustain, comfort and console.

The soul realizes
there must be an origin
whence comes this mighty stream,
inundating it, or a sun
whence proceeds this great light.
It never moves from its center
nor loses its peace,
which is Christ,
who gave His peace to the Apostles
in the first appearance after the Resurrection.

When the Lord says "Peace,"
it is more than a greeting;
His words are like acts wrought in us,
and must produce the effect He intends,
so that in those already prepared for it,
who are ready to put away everything corporal,
the soul is left in a state of pure spirituality,
so that it may be joined to the Uncreated Spirit
in this heavenly union.
For the Lord will fill our souls with himself
in the measure in which
we empty ourselves of all that is of this earth.
This is what the Lord meant when,
at the Last Supper,
He asked that they, the Apostles,
should become one with the Father,
and with Him,
even as He is in the Father,
and the Father in Him;
He asked, not only for the Apostles,
but for us all;
"for all who believe in me" (John 17:20, 23).

In this Mansion,
the soul seems subject
to none of the usual movements
of the faculties and the imagination,
which injure it and take away its peace.
It may seem to give the impression
that it is sure of its salvation,

and free from the risk of backsliding.
This is not so; it is sure of itself
only insofar
as it knows God is holding it by the hand
and it does not offend Him.
In fact
it has greater misgivings than before
and refrains more carefully
from committing the smallest offense
against God.
It longs to do more in God's service
and is afflicted at not being able to do this.
Its sense of obligation is heightened,
not lessened,
and this is a real penance;
and it is a great cross
when God takes away its health
so that it cannot do more penance.

The faculties and senses and passions
are not always in this state of peace,
though the soul itself is.
By contrast with the other Mansions,
nothing enters the soul to disturb its peace.
The things the soul hears may cause it distress,
but the center of the soul is not touched
or disturbed;
there the King dwells.

3 The striking effects of this kind of prayer.

The little butterfly has died;
within her lives Christ.
The first effect on the soul of this kind of prayer
is self-forgetfulness.
She forgets there is any honor,
even that of heaven, reserved for her,
so entirely is she employed
in seeking God's honor.
She takes care of God's honor,
as He takes care of hers.
She has no desire to exist
except to add to God's honor and glory.
Not that she neglects to eat and sleep,
though these are a torment to her.

The second effect
is a great desire to suffer,
allied to an extreme longing
that the will of God be done,
not her own, even in this,
and a great peace of soul about suffering
or the lack of it.
When they are persecuted,
these souls have a great interior joy,
and much more peace than before.
They bear no ill-will,
and conceive a special love
for those who ill-treat them.
Their former desire to die
and to enjoy our Lord
now becomes a more earnest desire
to serve Him,

even to live a great many years,
to suffer the severest trials,
to help some souls;
so that their conception of glory
is now to be able in some way
to help the Crucified.
Though sometimes they may forget this
in their great longing to be with God,
they return to their former desire,
offering His Majesty their will to live
as the most costly oblation
they can give Him.
They have lost all fear of death.

These souls have marked detachment
from everything
and a desire to be always either alone
or busy with something
that is to some soul's advantage.
They have no aridities or interior trials,
only a tender remembrance of our Lord,
who awakens the soul if it is negligent
with an impulse that proceeds
from the interior of the soul.

It has a special realization
of God's tender care for us
in communing with us,
and of the way He keeps begging us
to dwell with Him.
All trials seem as nothing
in comparison with these gentle,
penetrating touches of His love.
The soul has certainty
about the genuineness of God's favor;
the senses have no part in this;
all is the Lord's doing
and his favors come quite independently
of the acts of the soul,
apart from its having committed itself
wholly to God.

God and the soul have fruition of each other
in the deepest silence and tranquillity.
The understanding does not stir,
or seek anything.
Not that the faculties are lost;
they do not work, but seem to be dazed.
The astonishing thing is that in this state
raptures hardly ever occur.
No longer do devotional images,
sermons, music, and the like,
send them into raptures,
or lead to suspension of the senses;
this weakness has left them.

The Lord himself has greatly strengthened,
dilated and equipped the soul
by His companionship.
It is now
that the bride receives the kiss of the Bridegroom
for which she has been longing.
Here the wounded heart
receives waters in abundance,
here the soul delights in the tabernacle of God.

The thought that it might lose this great blessing
only makes the soul walk more warily,
and it is careful not to lose
any opportunity of pleasing God better.
In fact, the more such souls are favored by God,
the more fearful they become,
being now aware,
because of their closeness to God,
of the seriousness of their sins
and their own wretchedness.
Now they wish life to come to an end,
now they are anxious to live longer
in order to serve God in love.
There is no lack of crosses,
but they are not disturbed by them,
and they do not lose their peace.
The storms pass quickly,

fair weather returns,
and the presence of the Lord within them
makes them forget everything.

4 Our Lord's aim in granting this favor; Martha and Mary must walk together.

The effects which have been described
are not invariably present all the time;
sometimes our Lord leaves such souls
to their own nature,
but only for a short time.
Some chance happening
may cause turmoil in the soul
but the Lord gives it great determination,
so that it will not turn from Him,
but increases its good resolutions to be steadfast.
It is our Lord's will
thus to let the soul realize what it is;
to humble it,
that it may better realize what it owes to God.

It must not be imagined
that these souls are altogether free
from imperfections, or even from venial sins;
they are not, either, proof against mortal sin,
though as far as they know
they are free from it.
It distresses them
that so many souls are lost,
and when they recall those
whom Scripture describes
as highly favored by the Lord, like Solomon,
they cannot but be afraid.
"Blessed is the man that feareth God";
we must not feel sure of ourselves.

These favors are not given
merely to give the soul pleasure;

they are given to strengthen our weakness,
so that we may be able to imitate Christ
in His sufferings;
and this is the greatest thing
God can do for us:
grant us a life which is in imitation
of that lived by our Lord.

We always find that those who walked
closest to Christ our Lord
had to bear the greatest trials.
This was so of His blessed Mother
and the Apostles.
In the life of St. Paul
we see the effects of genuine visions
and of contemplation;
he did not shut himself up with his visions
but took not a day's rest,
and had to endure terrible trials.
And what did St. Peter do
when our Lord told him to return to Rome?
He went straight to his death,
which was a great mercy for him.

A soul in which our Lord makes His special abode
will never think of itself, or of honors.
It will think only of pleasing Him
and showing how it loves Him.
This is the aim of prayer;
this is the purpose of the spiritual marriage,
of which are born
good works and good works alone.

Such works are the sign of every genuine favor
and of everything else that comes from God.
Our good resolutions in prayer
must be borne out in good works;
prayer should teach us
to subdue our own will.
If we fix our eyes on the Crucified,
nothing else will be of much importance.

His Majesty suffered so much for love of us;
how can we expect to please Him
by words alone?

Do you know
when people become really spiritual?
When they become the slaves of God
and are branded with His sign,
which is the sign of the Cross,
in token that they have given Him their freedom.
They may be sold by Him as slaves,
slaves of the whole world,
as He was himself.
Unless they resolve to do this,
they need not expect to make progress.
For the foundation of the whole edifice
is humility,
and if they are not humble,
the Lord will not wish them
to reach any great height.

So, to lay good foundations,
wish to be the least of all,
be a slave to God,
and find ways of serving your companions.
I repeat that you must not build
upon the foundation of prayer
and contemplation alone,
for unless you strive after the virtues,
and practice them,
you will never grow to be more than dwarfs.
Love can never be content
to stay long where it is,
and we must go forward, or go back.

The only repose these souls enjoy
is of an interior kind;
of outward repose they get less and less,
since the soul is fighting harder
to keep the faculties and senses,
and everything to do with the body,

from being idle, than it did when before.
Only now does it realize, as never before,
the great gain to be derived from trials,
which may have been
the means whereby God brought it
to this state;
nor did it previously realize
how the companionship it now enjoys
would give it much greater strength
than it ever had before.
It cannot be doubted that we gain strength
through the most sovereign union
of spirit with Spirit.

The body is strengthened, too,
by an overflow of strength from the soul.
We should decide to engage in prayer,
not for our enjoyment,
but to acquire strength
which fits us for service.
We should not try to receive favors from God
by any other means
than that used by Him and by all the Saints.
Martha and Mary must work together,
and Mary needs her sister's help
besides the presence of Jesus.
The better part came to Mary
only in the bearing of trials,
and the martyrdom of witnessing the Lord's death,
not to speak of the suffering of His absence.
She was not always
in the delights of contemplation at the Lord's feet.

You may be tempted to think that,
being unable to teach and preach,
you do not know how to bring souls to God.
We must serve the Lord
in ways which are within our power,
not have ambitious desires
which are impossible to attain,
and sometimes come from the devil.

Show great humility and mortification,
be the servants of all,
and show great charity;
have a fervent love of our Lord,
constantly awakening the zeal of your sisters
by your virtues.
These things you really can do,
and this is a very great service to God.
If by your example
your sisters become better,
then they will praise God better,
and pray better for their neighbors.

We must not build towers without foundations
and the Lord does not look so much
at the magnitude of what we do,
as at the love with which we do it.
Let us not grow weary
in offering the Lord,
during the whole of this short life,
whatever interior or exterior sacrifice
we are able to make,
and His Majesty will offer it
with that which He made to the Father
for us on the Cross.
In this way we realize
that the value of the act is in the will,
not in its importance.

May it please His Majesty
to bring us all to meet
where we may praise Him
through the merits of His Son,
Amen.

Jesus

Remember that no one can enter these Mansions by his own efforts.
The Lord is a great lover of humility,
and if you consider yourselves unworthy
of entering even the Third Mansion,
He will more quickly
give you the will to enter the Fifth,
and if He should bring you
into the last Mansions
you will find rest in everything,
even in the things which most try you.

There are many more Mansions
besides those I have described here,
in which you will want to lose yourselves
in praise of the great God who created you
in His own image and likeness.

I submit all here written,
to the judgment of the Holy Roman
Catholic Church,
in which I wish to live and die.
Amen.